CAMBRIDGE LIBRARY COLLECTION

Books of enduring scholarly value

Anthropology

The first use of the word 'anthropology' in English was recorded in 1593, but its modern use to indicate the study and science of humanity became current in the late nineteenth century. At that time a separate discipline had begun to evolve from many component strands (including history, archaeology, linguistics, biology and anatomy), and the study of so-called 'primitive' peoples was given impetus not only by the reports of individual explorers but also by the need of colonial powers to define and classify the unfamiliar populations which they governed. From the ethnographic writings of early explorers to the 1898 Cambridge expedition to the Torres Straits, often regarded as the first truly 'anthropological' field research, these books provide eye-witness information on often vanished peoples and ways of life, as well as evidence for the development of a new scientific discipline.

The Kachins

Ola Hanson (1864–1927) was a Swedish-American missionary from Minnesota, posted to northern Burma in 1890. He lived with the Kachin people and became fluent in their language, compiling a word-list and eventually producing a Kachin–English dictionary. Their own culture and complex belief system were orally transmitted: Hanson therefore devised an alphabetical transcription for his translation of the Bible into Kachin, and this writing system later became widespread in Burma. First published in 1913, this book was written after Hanson had lived with the Kachins for over twenty years, and offers a unique insight into their culture at this time. It outlines their origins, dialects, law and weapons, as well as the details of Kachin religious beliefs and ceremonies for births, marriage and death. This book is valuable as both an ethnography of the Kachin people and as an example of the perspective of an early twentieth-century missionary.

Cambridge University Press has long been a pioneer in the reissuing of out-of-print titles from its own backlist, producing digital reprints of books that are still sought after by scholars and students but could not be reprinted economically using traditional technology. The Cambridge Library Collection extends this activity to a wider range of books which are still of importance to researchers and professionals, either for the source material they contain, or as landmarks in the history of their academic discipline.

Drawing from the world-renowned collections in the Cambridge University Library and other partner libraries, and guided by the advice of experts in each subject area, Cambridge University Press is using state-of-the-art scanning machines in its own Printing House to capture the content of each book selected for inclusion. The files are processed to give a consistently clear, crisp image, and the books finished to the high quality standard for which the Press is recognised around the world. The latest print-on-demand technology ensures that the books will remain available indefinitely, and that orders for single or multiple copies can quickly be supplied.

The Cambridge Library Collection brings back to life books of enduring scholarly value (including out-of-copyright works originally issued by other publishers) across a wide range of disciplines in the humanities and social sciences and in science and technology.

The Kachins

Their Customs and Traditions

Ola Hanson

CAMBRIDGE UNIVERSITY PRESS

Cambridge, New York, Melbourne, Madrid, Cape Town,
Singapore, São Paolo, Delhi, Mexico City

Published in the United States of America by Cambridge University Press, New York

www.cambridge.org
Information on this title: www.cambridge.org/9781108046091

This edition first published 1913
This digitally printed version 2012

ISBN 978-1-108-04609-1 Paperback

Bridge over the Paknoi Hka boundary between Burma and China.

Frontispiece. *Illustrations from photos by Rev. G. J. Geis.*

THE KACHINS

THEIR CUSTOMS AND TRADITIONS

BY

Rev. O. HANSON, Litt. D.

RANGOON:

AMERICAN BAPTIST MISSION PRESS

F. D. PHINNEY, SUPT.

1913

CONTENTS.

IX. Social Life and Amusements.

Children at Play. Women. Young people. The village bard. Music. Dance and dancing. The great religious dance. (*manau*). The death-dance.

X. Intellectual Development.

Kachins illiterate. Sign-language. Drawing. Calendar. Measures. Weights. Money. Numbers. Plants and medicines. Proverbs. Riddles.

XI. Mythology and Traditions.

Creation. Flood. Origin of death. The lost book. Why the Kachins are nat-worshippers. Explanation of natural phenomena. Thunder. The rainbow. Eclipses. Earthquake. The moon. The universe. Origin of the religious dance. First man to die of snake-bite. How fire was discovered. First man burned to death. Customs observed after a fire. First men killed by accident. First man drowned. Why the Kachins offer to the spirit of jealousy. How rice was obtained. How water was found.

XII. In quest of the Unknown.

Attempts to disclose the secrects of the future. The medium. The diviner. Divination. Auguries. Omens, dreams. Charms. Rules to insure good luck. Ordeals. Witchcraft. "Cursing."

XIII. The Kachin Religion.

Spirit-worship. Reticence regarding details. Ancestor worship Universality of spirits. Dread of the nats. No trace of totemism. the priest-hood. *Jaiwa, Dumsa, Hpunglum.* Offerings. Nat-altars. The nat. Primitive nats. Of later date. Ancestral spirits. Fates. Witch-nats. Fear the motive power in their religion. Propitiation of the nats. Objects sought. Order of service. Appeasing offended nats. Warding off danger. Prayers for riches. Sowing and harvest festivals. Help in illness. Ideas of a supreme being. No worship in his honor.

XIV. Natal Ceremonies.

Large families desired. Rules observed at child-birth. Cutting of the navel. Natal feast. Purification of the mother. Death in confinement. Names and naming. "Nick-names." General remarks.

XV. Marriage Ceremonies.

Courtship. Parents arranging the details. Consanguinity Abduction. Preliminaries. Proposal. Price paid. Bride leaving the parental home. Presents exchanged. Marriage ceremony. Blessing the bride. Testing her mind. Work of the *Jaiwa.* Return of the bridal party. Bride visiting her parental home.

INTRODUCTION.

In publishing this volume on the Kachins, I present the results of many years of study and contact with this interesting people. I have visited them in almost every part of Kachinland, from Assam, the Hukong Valley and the confluence of the Măli and N-Mai rivers, to the southernmost part of the Northern Shan States. Among the Kachins in Chinese territory very little original work has been done, but we are sure that in regard to life, customs and religion they are practically one with their kinsmen to the west.

The book makes no claim to be exhaustive, especially in regard to detailed accounts of religious customs and traditional lore. Two or three volumes of this size would not suffice if we should attempt minute details and a full collection of all their stories. Every community exhibits some peculiarities in regard to religious practices; they may have their own local "divinities" attending to their special needs, receiving honor in some particular way There is no particular gain in following out all these details, as they after all bear the marks of what is recognized as the general religious customs and ceremonies. Stories and traditions have also local colourings and it is proverbial that priests and story-tellers do not agree among themselves. What we here attempt is to present the Kachin as he appears in his everyday life in his mountain home, and an account of his customs and religion as far as they are common and accepted by all.

Our principal source of information regarding the hill-tribes is the "Gazetteer of Upper Burma and the Shan States." This is an excellent work representing a vast amount of labour. I have not made it a point to criticize or correct the account of the Kachins there given. Only a few times have I quoted from its pages, where in so doing I am enabled to bring out my own view more clearly. I have preferred to tell my own story, as I have it from the life of the Kachins, and from a long observation of their village and homelife. Those particularly interested in the subject can easily find out where we differ or agree. Having followed this course, it does not mean that I do not heartily appreciate what has been done by others. The account as given in the Gazetteer is quite full, and remarkably exact for the time it was written; and the compilers, who generally had to depend on the assistance of interpreters, did their work wonderfully well.

The temptation has been strong to compare the Kachin customs and religion with the practices of related tribes such as the Karens, Chins, Nagas, Garos, Mishmis and Abors. The Assam Census Report of 1891 is particularly a great storehouse furnished with material for ethnological study, and most of the border tribes there described have a great deal in common. But in a work of this kind it is best to confine ourselves to the particular people under survey. When monographs of all the principal tribes and races are before us, someone will settle down to the inviting task of giving us a comprehensive view of the whole field.

The chapter on the Origin of the Kachins will probably seem too radical, as it goes contrary to many generally accepted ideas of the Kachin communal life. We are probably not ready to drop the word "tribes" when speaking of the five ruling families. But to show how this simplifies matters let me quote from the Gazetteer, page 402, Chap. VII. Speaking about family names the author says: "It is somewhat singular that all having the same surname, whether they belong to the same or different tribes, regard themselves of one blood and do not intermarry. Thus a Maran *Chumlut* cannot take a wife from the Szi *Chumlut.* This is interesting, because it suggests totemism, and because it shows that the family distinctions are older than the tribal." The author of these sentences came near stumbling on the true solution of the problem. A *Chamlut* is a *Chamlut* under whatever chief he may live, and cannot marry anyone with that name. The fact that he is the subject of a Măran or Lăhpai chief does not in the least interfere with his family relations. He is not a Măran or Lăhpai, simply a *Chamlut* who may at any time move and settle down in a village ruled by a Mărip, Nhkum or Lăhtaw chief. It is quite true that "family distinctions are older than the tribal." To the Kachin mind there is nothing but family distinctions, however involved they may seem to us. If we, for the sake of convenience, still use the word "tribe" to distinguish the ruling families in their capacities as chieftains, we should not forget that the family of a chief is no more a "tribe" than is the family of any other name. In this work, however, I have avoided the use of the word because of the confusion it has caused.

In tracing three different movements in the Kachin advance south I am relying on vague hints in their traditions, and on statements of a few old men whose opinions have seemed to me worthy of consideration. If my memory does not fail me, the first one who put me on this track was an old Gauri chief of Măhtim, one of the most intelligent Kachins I have ever seen.

In a supplement I have tried to elucidate the intricate question of Kachin relationship and family names. Those that wish to pursue these studies further will find some help from the Kachin Dictionary and Grammar. The original of many of the stories and traditions given in these pages will be found in the Kachin Spelling Book and First Reader.

Those who have come in contact with the Kachins

will no doubt have in mind many particulars not mentioned in these pages. My aim has been to present the essential features that will interest the ethnologist and the student of language and comparative religion, and give a practical working knowledge of Kachin ways, habits and customs.

O. H.

Namkham, Northern Shan States,
August, 1912.

THE KACHINS

THEIR CUSTOMS AND TRADITIONS.

CHAPTER I.

THE ORIGIN OF THE KACHINS.

The Kachins occupy a large and fertile territory extending from 29° north latitude to almost 23° north latitude. They are a mountain people, and it is only recently that some of them have taken to the plains, where they, however, rapidly degenerate or lose their peculiar characteristics. Most of them live within the boundaries of British Burma, but large numbers inhabit the hill-country of western Yunnan, and smaller communities are found in Assam and along the borders of Tibet. The whole of northern Burma down to the 24th parallel is largely under Kachin influence. On the west side of the Irrawaddy they are not as strongly represented as on the east, but they are found as far south as Katha and Wuntho, holding the hills in the Mogaung district, and in undisputed possession of the country north of Kamaing, the Jade-mines, and the whole of the Hukong valley. The hill-tract between Myitkyina and the Kampti valley is inhabited by the Hkahku Kachins, and the Singhpo families are still numerous on the north-east border of Assam. On the east of the great artery they hold both mountains and valleys as far as the Salween, and are quite numerous as far south as North Hsenwi and the Ruby-mines district. Formerly the large plains in the Bhamo district and northern Shan States were also tributary to them. The Kachin chief lived in his mountain "fortress," from which he sent his subordinates to collect taxes or levy blackmail on the Shans and Burmans in the lowlands. If there was any delay in payment, or if they showed any spirit of insubordination, the robber-chief took quick vengeance, raiding their villages or imposing a heavy fine in grain, cattle and money. It is only the British rule that has put an end to their conquests, and established peace and order among the hills.

The Assam Kachins. The *Singhpo* of Assam is the same as the *Jinghpaw* or Kachin of Burma. The Assamese being unable to pronounce the word *Jinghpaw,* render it *Singhpaw.* The true *Singhpaw* is in most particulars one with his kinsmen further south, and in former days there was a great deal more intercommunication than there is now between the two sections. There are also some small families such as the *Dărungs* and *Faqueers* who speak *Singhpo,* but are of mixed blood. Pure *Singhpos* (Kachins) are found east of Ledo, and the dialect is spoken as far west as Dibrugarh and Golaghat. The *Dărungs* have a story that they were for generations held as slaves by the Dărung river in the Hukong valley, when the Shans (no doubt under the rule of the Ahoms), ruled that country. Thus their dialect became largely a Shan patois, and they lost many of their Kachin characteristics. There is apparently some truth in this, and the Ahom rule is no doubt responsible for the fact that the Kachins never became so strong on the west side of the Irrawaddy as on the east.

Kachins in China. In western Yunnan the Atsi Kachins are very numerous and further north are found the Mărus, Nungs, and other allied tribes, of which very little is known. When more has been learned regarding the frontier tribes we will know more about the race as a whole and their past movements. We know, however, that in language, habits, customs and religion they do not materially differ from their kinsmen in other parts of Kachinland.

Kachin tribes. There are, strictly speaking, no Kachin tribes. They themselves recognize only different families and linguistic divisions. For the sake of convenience, however, we may call the group of families that speak the same dialect a tribe or a clan, while we employ the name Kachin for the people as a whole. Still it must be remembred that the linguistic and family divisions are not at all co-terminous. Following the linguistic divisions we have the *Jinghpaw, Măru, Lăshi, Atsi,* and *Nung* tribes, while the *Hkaku, Gauri* and *Săsan* simply represent local conditions. All Kachins, however, whatever dialect they speak, call themselves *Jinghpaw,* and recognize a common source and ancestry. Most of them know nothing about the word Kachin, and, those that do as a rule resent the appellation, as carrying with it an unpleasant reference to their barbarous and uncivilized ways. But we accept the term because it is in common use, and is the only name in which all these divisions and subdivisions can be included. The Yawyin or Lishaw tribe are by some Kachins claimed as distant relatives, and many of them live within Kachin territory, but they prefer to regard themselves as an offshoot from the Chinese, and in this they are undoubtedly correct.

Origin of Kachin Families. According to Kachin tradition, (our only authority on the subject), they are the descendants of a certain *Wahkyet wa,* a semi-mythological figure. His five oldest sons became the progenitors of the five recognized families of chieftains. These are—

La N-Gam, (Mărip wa Gumja), the "golden" father of the *Mărip* family.

La N-Naw, (Lăhtaw wa Naw Lawn), the "aggressive" father of the *Lăhtaws.*

La N-La, (Lăhpai wa La Tsan), the "far-spreading" father of the *Lăhpais.*

La N-Tu, (*Tsit wa Tu Hkum*), the "verdant" and growing father of the *N-Hkums.*

La N-Tang, (*Măran wa Ningshawng*), the "first" of the *Mărans.*

From these five families come all the hereditary chiefs, and no one bearing one or the other of these names can ever be counted among the "commoners." When a branch of a chief's family "loses caste" and dwindles down among the common people, the original name and all that goes with it is lost. (See Supplement II).

Following these five were born three younger sons, who did not become rulers. Their families became identified with and absorbed in the three smallest of the first five, thus helping to swell their numbers. These are—

La N-Yaw, who became one with the *N-Hkum* family.

La N-Hka, who became identified with the *Lăhtaws,* his particular descendants becoming known as the *Lăhtaw Hka shu Hka sha,* the divided children of the *Lăhtaws.*

La N-Kying, "the branch" who abode with the *Măran* family, his children being given the name *Măran wa Kying Nang,* the "outgrowing" branches of the *Mărans.*" Individuals from these families may also become chiefs, but are not reckoned in dignity with the regular chieftains.

According to one tradition, *Wahkyet wa* had three wives, according to other sources ten times that number. The first of these, *Măgawng Kăbang Măjan,* is apparently the mother of the chiefs, although this is not quite certain. The other wives became the mothers of the numerous families of "commoners," (*dăroi dărat*), who are ruled by the chiefs from the ruling families. These can never carry the name of a chief except in the sense that they are his slaves, dependants or subjects. A *Lăhpai* chief, for instance, will rule over a village where there are represented scores and scores of common families. The custom of naming such a community after the chief naturally gave rise to the impression that the chief and his subjects were of the same "tribe," while in reality the common people bear the name of the chieftain only by courtesy or as a matter of convenience. There can be no blood relation between them.

Ancestral Home. Where are we to look for the ancestral home of *Wahkyet wa* and his valiant sons? If we could answer this question with absolute certainty we would bring light on many an obscure point in early Burman history. But here we are left to often contradictory traditions and consequent conjectures. There are, however, three faint beacon lights to guide us in this sea of uncertainty. (1) All Kachins claim that they come from *Mǎjoi Shingra Bum* or *Kǎang Shingra;* (2) their traditions indicate an acquaintance with the sources of the Irrawaddy, and (3) the names of the "original" districts ruled by the first ancestral chiefs have been handed down to us.

It would seem that with these landmarks to guide us we would be able to determine something regarding their early home. But a close examination leads to the disappointing conclusion that we are only dealing with legends from which very little of a historical character can be extracted, and where we seem to have history it leads us only two or three centuries back. Our first question is where to locate *Mǎjoi Shingra Bum,* or as it is also called, *Kǎang Shingra* or *Mǎjoi Shingra Hkindawt.* The meaning of the words are fairly plain. The only question is what interpretation to give to the word *Shingra.* It may mean level, even, or original and thus common. In either case the meaning would be clear. It is "the naturally flat (or original) mountain," the "central (or common) plain," the "borders of the common plain." In each case we have the picture of a plateau or high table-land, the ancestral home, situated at the centre of the world, being the border land to all surrounding countries. All Kachins when confronted with the question where this mountain is to be found, invariably reply, "Way up there," pointing to the north. Further than this they cannot carry us. A few will describe a high, snowclad mountain reminding us of *Dapha Bum* in north-eastern Assam. That the old Kachins were acquainted with this noble hill is quite certain, and the word *bum* is the Kachin for mountain. But to-day it lingers in their tradition as a kind of Mount Meru. Others claim that it is a land of snow and frost, much colder than any place now inhabited by them. Here too we deal most likely with mere conjectures and impressions. The Kachins have no term for snow, while they have a word for frost which they see every cold season among their present hills. Even a northern Kachin must borrow a Chinese term when naming a snow-drift. Some of the Hukong Kachins locate the mountain in the territory occupied by the *Nungs,* north-east of Kamhti Long. That they occupied this district for some time on their way south is certain, but it cannot have been their original home.

While an acquaintance with the head-waters of the Irrawaddy is evident, it does not throw much light on our enquiry. Four great rivers are mentioned in the old traditions. The are the *Măli hka* (the Irrawaddy), called in poetic language *Ja Kăw,* the golden female *Kaw,* which was "measured out" (by the Creator) with a golden spoon; no doubt a reference to the well known fact that gold has always been washed in this river; the *N-Mai hka;* (the *N-Mai* river), called figuratively *Ja Lu,* the golden *Lu,* sister to the *Măli hka* (another rendering makes the *N-Mai* the wife of the *Măli*), measured out with a silver spoon; the general belief is that the *N-Mai* produces silver as the *Măli* gold; the *N-Shawn,* (probably the *Dihing*) regarded as a male "measured out" with a copper spoon, and the *Hpunggawn* (most likely the *Brahmaputra*), of the same gender and humble origin. All that can be safely inferred from the mention of these names is that the Kachin hordes two or three centuries ago were living in the territory drained by these great arteries. They could not for some time break through the barrier that kept them back beyond the 28th parallel. Only as the Shan power in Assam and Yunnan began to weaken could the warriors press south. But that they lived in this region probably for centuries, does not prove that this was actually their ancestral home. This was their "wilderness" where they were trained for the second and most important advance.

When we examine the names of the original districts ruled by the five parent chiefs, and try to identify them with present localities, we find that these record the memories of the first conquests after they have left the north Kamhti country, and thus lead us back only about two hundred and fifty or three hundred years. Here as elsewhere tradition is not unanimous, but the most likely version is that, (1) "The golden father of the *Mărips* ruled the *Wang Ya*, the round plain, which may refer to the Hukong where the *Mărips* are numerous; (2) the "aggressive ruler" of the *Lăhtaws* occupied the *Jaw Man Jaw Hkang,* which may be a strip of *Naga* land in north-eastern Assam, or the hills east of the *Măli hka,* up to then held by Burmans and Chins; (3) the "far-spreading" *Lăhpai* ruled the large *Tawn Singkawng* district, probably identical with the *Singkawng* Hills in the *Hkahku* country; (4) the "verdant and growing" father of the *N-Hkums,* held sway in the *Tsit ga,* the green country, or as some pronounce it, *Tsin ga,* the cool, pleasant land, probably the Kamhti valley; and (5) the "first" of the *Mărans* ruled the *Gumshu Gumwa,* the sugarcane district, a tract of land still bearing that name in the *Hkahku* hills. If our indentification is in any way correct, it is plain that we here deal with conditions as they existed two and a half or three centuries ago. We can feel fairly sure that just about this must have been the colouring of the Kachin map at that time.

What we can learn from our three landmarks may now be summed up in a few words. For centuries the *Jinghpaw* families had been living on the border land between Assam, China and northern Burma. When they first occupied that territory is mere conjecture. There they lived and multiplied, always eager to break through the wall and occupy the land further south. But the "naturally level mountain" cannot be located here, and we must look still further

2

north for the birth-place of the race. This must be sought among the highlands of Mongolia, and on the border land of eastern Tibet and western Szchuan. Here stood the cradle not only of the Kachins, but also of the Burmans and other Mongolian tribes. At a remote period the Burmans began to move south and laid the foundation of mighty kingdoms. Later smaller tribes like the Chins, Nagas, Lahus and possibly Karens followed in the wake, our Kachins holding a central position. The Naga tribes following the Patkoi range settled down among these high hills, gradually taking possession of more and more of the Yoma range where the Burmans were only periodically strong. The Lahus and Karens keeping to the east of the Salween, seem to have been permitted to move peacefully southward. But the Jinghpaws in the centre, aiming for more valuable acquisitions, were for a long time kept back by the strong Shan rulers in Assam and Yunnan. They were compelled to live in the land of the "four rivers" until opportunity again presented itself for the new advance. It is from this period that our traditions and stories mainly date. As the Yunnan Shans lost their grip and the Ahom kings became weak, the Kachins began to move. They carried with them the memories of their second home, and through them ring a few faint echoes of a still earlier date and home. But it is from the time of their second advance that we can follow their movements with a certain amount of precision and accuracy.

The name Kachin. If we could tell with certainty how and when the name Kachin originated, there would be at least one fixed point in their history. But unfortunately this is not possible. We can be sure of this only, that it is a Burmese appellation, not known in either Assam or China, but in use in Upper Burma early in the last century. The well known traveler and missionary Dr. Kincaid, in the year 1837, come in contact with the "*Ka Khyens*" around Mogaung, being under the impression that "they are of the same race as the Karens." As already stated all Kachins call themselves Jinghpaw, but just as the Tai race became known as Shan, the Braginyaw tribes as Karens, the Jinghpaws were called Kachin. The Shans and Palaungs call them *Hkang*, the same name the Kachins give to the Chins, an opprobrious term indicating mixed race and parentage. The Chinese call them *Ye Jein*, wild men, which in Kachin becomes *Yawyin* and is applied to the Lishaws. The Burmans must have had their first information regarding the advancing Kachins from the Shans and Chinese. In some way they coined the term in accordance with the names employed by them. The *Hkang* of the Shan and the *Jein* of the Chinese may for short have become *Hka Khyen*, or *Ka Khyen*, which seems to have been the earliest way of pronouncing and spelling the word. This again has been simplified to our "Kachin." This seems to me the simplest and most natural explanation. The meaning proposed that we have in the name the Burmese words for sour (ခါး) and bitter (ချဉ်) is possible, but not at all probable. If this is the etymology, then we have in this name a reference to the savage state of the rude mountaineers. A theory advanced by some Kachins is that we have in the word a combination of the Kachin and Burmese words for basket (*ka* and ခြင်း *hkyin*). Thus there would be a reference to the fact that a Kachin is never seen on the road without carrying a basket. This is probably as good a derivation as any other, but no better. My own preference is for the first explanation, as the most natural and the most likely. The word Jinghpaw, which is the racial name, is sometimes used in the sense of man (*homo*), but this meaning is now almost lost, even in the antiquated religious language, where another term has been introduced. But this is the word that should be used in addressing the Kachins. This is recognized by all, while the term Kachin, like the Shan word *Hkang*, and the Chinese *Ye Jein*, is unknown by most, and resented by those that have given any thought to its meaning.

Migrations. Guided by the traditions referred to, and the possibilities they suggest, we will be able to form an idea of the Kachin conquest of northern Burma and adjacent territory. We need go back about 250 or 300 years to come in contact with the comparatively small groups of Jinghpaw families as they break up from their mountain homes around the great rivers to the north of the Kamhti, where they have lived since their first advance from the "Central Plain." They made themselve felt among the northern Shans and to this day the Kamhti and Assam Shans speak Kachin, while few of the southern Shans can boast this accomplishment. More than once they attacked Sadiya during the reign of the later Ahom kings; they proved useful allies to the Burmans, who at the beginning of the late century entered Assam through the Patkoi pass and helped to overthrow the Ahom kingdom. Before that time detachments of them had been in the service of the Ahom kings. At other times they would be on unfriendly terms with the Shans and there would be fierce raiding and fighting on the Assam frontier. But the Jinghpaws never gained a strong foot-hold in Assam, and thus they turned south and east, overrunning the Kamhti valley, and crossing the Patkoi range, practically exterminated the Hukong population. Only a few Shans remain there to this day, all of them subjects to the Kachins. This happened probably about two hundred years ago. Having obtained a foot-hold, the conquest of the whole region between the Kamhti and Hukong valleys, as far south as to the Mogaung river, followed in due time. The Shans and Burmans were driven out, and only the ruins of their pagodas, the trees planted around their monastaries, and the names of their villages remained to tell the story of fierce fighting and wholesale slaughter. A few were captured and held as slaves, but all that could fled south for protection among their kinsmen. Having advanced as far south as the Mogaung and Katha districts, they encountered more organized resistance and found further progress in that direction impossible. They consequently turned east and looked for new conquest among the hills on the other side of the Irrawaddy. Crossing the river north of Myitkyina they soon became masters of the whole country between the Irrawaddy and the Salween, except that they were unable to hold the valleys ruled by the Chinese. The La, Shan, Palaung and Chinese hill-population receded further and further south, and most of the villages remain on the old sites of the Tai people. The rich Shan valleys became tributaries to the mountain chiefs, and had it not been for the British occupation many of them would have shared the fate of the Hukong.

When the main body of the Jinghpaws left their home north of the Kamhti and took possession of the country west of the Irrawaddy, smaller detachments, mostly represented by the *Mărus,* forced their way southward between the Măli and Nmai rivers. But they were never strong enough to gain much headway south of the Nmai. It was only after their kinsmen, the Jinghpaws, had crossed the Irrawaddy and become powerful enough to invade the region north of the Taiping that the Mărus could seek new homes. They pushed down along the Chinese frontier and many of them settled among the Jinghpaws. Thus we find Măru villages and communities scattered all over the hills. While of the same parent stock as the Jinghpaws they show in their speech a remarkable relationship to the Burmese. In customs and religion they are, however, true Kachins, with some peculiarities of their own. A large number of them came under the influence of the strong Lăhpai family and by intermarriage a new clan grew up, the Atsi. These developed a new dialect and some of their customs differ somewhat from both Jinghpaw and Măru, but in the main they are true Kachins. Their speech, as is natural, is very closely related to the Măru. Through the Atsis, by intermarriage with the Mărans, and probably Chinese, came the Lăshis, the youngest of the distinct divisions, unless the Săsans be so regarded, which, as already indicated, seems unnecessary. The Lăshi shows in his dialect his Măru parentage, but in certain other respects gives evidence of the more modern conditions under which he has grown up. Thus the Măru, Atsi and Lăshi are practically the same people, and their dialects are only modifications of the same language. As it is only by the help of their stronger kinsmen that they have been able to secure territory, they have always, so to speak, been kept to the backwoods, and are thus less civilized and if possible more superstitious than the regular Jinghpaws.

Relation between Măru and Burmese. While the Mărus, or as they call themselves, the Lawng Waw, belong to the Jinghpaw family, the marked similarity between the Măru dialects (including Atsi and Lăshi) to the Burmese indicates an interesting condition in early history. It is questionable, however, if their dialects taken as a whole stand any nearer Burmese than does Jinghpaw. One fourth of the roots are identical in Jinghpaw and Burmese; grammar and constructions are practically the same. It is doubtful if more than this can be said of the Măru group. Still the fact that quite a number of their words retain the Burman ring, where Jinghpaw has adopted new terms or changed the old so as to be almost unrecognizable, indicates a closer relationship in the distant past between the Mărus and Burmans than between the Jinghpaws and Burmans. The earliest home of all the tribes of Burma was no doubt the same. The Burmans were the first to push south. They were probably followed by the Lahus and the Karens. Centuries later they were followed by Chins, Nagas, Jinghpaws and Mărus. The Chins and Jinghpaws kept to the west of the Irrawaddy, while the Mărus came down on the east side, where they came in contact with such Burmese settlements as had been able to maintain themselves north of the Nmai. But the more aggressive and numerous Burmans soon left their weaker brethren and pushed on to more promising fields. Then in the course of time northern Burma came under Shan influence. The

Shan kings of Tali and Assam kept the Mărus and Jinghpaws in the territory already indicated. The Jinghpaws to the west were more in touch with the outside world than the now isolated Mărus. While the latter retained some early characteristics of speech, they ran easily into brogues among their lonely hills and valleys. The Jinghpaws in touch with the larger life modified their speech, but maintained the unity of their dialect. Thus when the day came for a new advance south, the Jinghpaws had the advantage of the larger and more liberal training, and being united by a common dialect, were in a position where they could act with unity of purpose.

Territorial Divisions. If our story of the Kachins, as we have outlined it in the foregoing pages, is anywhere nearly correct, it takes on an historical character from the day they began their second advance, leaving their homes at the head-waters of the Irrawaddy, forcing their way into Assam, Burma and Yunnan. What movements there were before that time from a region still further north we can only conjecture. The territorial distribution of the families today indicates the position they held two or three centuries ago. But changes were constantly taking place during the time the Kachins were independent and at liberty to acquire new territory by conquest. As we take a glance at the Kachin map of today we find in the far north-east the Nungs (Hka Nungs, as they are called by the Shans). They are a degenerate branch of a once strong and intelligent tribe. Many of them are slaves to the Kamhti Shans, and their general appearance is low, cringing and savage. To the west of them we have the Singhpos of Assam. They are in all essentials one with their kinsmen further north and south, but lacking in some of their stronger qualities. They exhibit both in speeeh and customs a strong Shan influence, and a few of them have accepted a form of Buddhism while still retaining many of their own religious practices. Still moving south we meet the Hkahkus along the west bank of the Irrawaddy. The Hukong

Kachins, of which the Săsans have departed most widely from the parent stock, are closely related to them. South of these we come in contact with the main body of the race in the Myitkyina, Bhamo, Mogaung and Katha districts. In the Southern Shan States they hold the hills and goodly numbers are found in the Ruby Mines district.

As it often happens that the conquerors are intellectually conquered by their subjects, so to a certain extent it has happened here. The Kachins that remained on the west side of the Irrawaddy developed localisms in their speech, and many of them, as in the Hukong and Kamhti valleys, became strongely influenced by the Shans as to customs and religion. In many villages are found Buddhist shrines, and the old remains of pagodas and monastaries are kept "sacred" for fear of the spirits having their abode in them. Even their own nat-worship has been modified under the influence of Buddhist teaching. This is especially true of the Assam Kachins and those of the Hukong. The more isolated communities in the Hills also developed some special characteristics and peculiarities in dialect. Those along the west bank of the Irrawaddy in time became known as the Hkahku people, that is the "up-river people." Their dialect differs somewhat from ordinary Kachin, (Jinghpaw), but they are true Kachins and adhere strictly to the ancestral customs and traditions. As time passed on a great number of sectional names grew up, but the original family names and the identity of the ruling families have always been maintained. On the east of the Irrawaddy the Jinghpaw dialect has remained remarkably pure, and the old customs and traditions have been everywhere followed. It is only of late years that Shan influence has been felt in the northern Shan States and in Chinese territory.

The demarcation of the sections occupied by the five ruling families is difficult, as they are represented in all parts of the country. It is, however, of importance only as it helps us to follow their early line of advance. In those days the chiefs of the same family would act together in offensive and defensive warfare, but in time they separated and established themselves wherever there was an opportunity. But scattered as they are, it is possible to some extent to outline their early conquests and settlements. That the present situation does not in all particulars conform to the traditional divisions of the land that we have already considered, is just what we would expect.

The *Mărips* are found mostly on the west of the Irrawaddy. Their territory is, broadly speaking, the Hukong valley, the district around the jade mines, and parts of the Hkahku hills. Their first conquest is apparently the Hukong. Scattered families are today found in the whole of the Kachin land. This may be true of any family that we may mention.

The *Lăhtaws* have several villages in the Hukong. They are strong on both sides of the Irrawaddy north of the confluence. They are well represented in the Myitkyina district, and are numerous in some parts of Bhamo and North Hsenwi circles. They are more widely scattered than the Mărips and are next to the Lăhpais the most numerous.

The *Lăhpai* family is by far the largest and strongest of them all. They are found in the Mogaung district and to the east of Myitkyina. All the Atsis along the whole Chinese frontier, from Sadon to Kutkai and Lashio are ruled by Lăhpai chiefs. The Gauri villages east of Bhamo are held by them, while after a short break filled in with the Mărans, we meet them again in the Hpunggan and Găra hills. Smaller groups are encountered in the Southern Shan States and almost anywhere among the hills.

The *Nhkums* are scattered all along the Chinese frontier. They are probably the weakest of the five ruling families. They have a number of villages in the Mogaung district, some east of Bhamo, and are fairly numerous in North Hsenwi, particularily in the Mong Baw circle. Their earliest home seems to have been west of the Irrawaddy around the Kamhti valley.

The *Mărans,* like the Ahkums, are very much scattered. They are found around Sinbo, Mogaung and Katha. South-east of Bhamo the Sǎna and Laika groups have Mǎran chiefs, and the Laikas again appear along the Salween in the Northern Shan States. In the Mong Myit circle and down towards the Ruby Mines they are also found. They are in some respects the most refined and intelligent of all the Kachins, except some of the leading families in the Hukong valley.

CHAPTER II.

THE KACHIN DIALECTS.

Dialects beginning with localisms and provincialisms grow up easily in savage and primitive conditions. All that is needed is to confine a group of families within an environment where contact with the outside world is small or none at all, and within a few generations we have a new dialect. In Asia as well as in other parts of the world, illiterate and backward districts show peculiarities of speech in nearly every village and community. It is the written page, the common school and the daily press that gradually eliminate localisms and dialectical differences. Still we know with what tenacity local dialects maintain themselves even amidst modern conditions. Within the British Isles we have Irish and Welsh, and until quite recently Cornish, while in Germany we speak of High and Low German, not to mention the great number of provincialisms, some of them of marked peculiarities. Among the Kachins the same tendencies have been at work with the usual results. But the fact that we have different dialects to deal with, does not work the same hardships with the Kachin student, as among the Karens or Chins, where often villages quite close to each other do not understand each others' dialect and have no means of inter-communication. Among the Kachins the leading dialect, Jinghpaw, is understood by nearly all from the borders of Tibet to the extreme south. It is only some of the Mărus and Atsis, that either do not speak Jinghpaw at all, or know it very imperfectly. Kachins are as a rule good linguists and many of them speak five or six dialects fluently.

Dialects. The Kachin dialects worthy of special attention are, the *Jinghpaw, Măru, Atsi, Lăshi* and *Nung.* Such localisms as *Hkahku, Gauri,* and *Săsan* represent only special conditions, and need not be called different forms of speech. These five dialects, and if we so wish, their localisms, comprise with the Burman, Naga and Chin group, the Burman family of the Turanian or Polytonic class of languages. In their earliest form they were strictly monosyllabic and polytonic. Most of them are now in their agglutinative state, and in the process of development show a tendency to dispense with the tones. In Jinghpaw about one fourth of the vocabulary is still monosyllabic, the rest is mainly dissyllabic.

Grammar. The grammar of all the Kachin dialects agrees in the main with the Burmese and that of the Burmese family. At least one-fourth of the roots are identical. Constructions and idioms are practically the same. Now that the Jinghpaw has taken on a literary form, it will like Burmese dispense with the tones more and more. The instances where the tones are now of importance will be obviated in various ways, and the meaning will be made clear by the use of new combinations of words rather than by inflections. Declension and conjugations are in Jinghpaw expressed by an elaborate system of noun and verbal particles. There are still traces in Burmese of a similar system. Some of the Kachin groups, like the Gauri, have a tendency to drop some of the verbal particles, and as the Jinghpaw develops the general trend will be to dispense with most of these rather troublesome adjuncts. We have already mentioned the marked similarity between Măru, Atsi, Lăshi and Burmese. This extends both to grammar and vocabulary. I am convinced, however, that when we go far enough back we will find the Jinghpaw as closely related to the leading language of Burma as is the Măru group. So far only the surface similarity has had any attention. We must go deeper before we can give the final verdict.

Outside Influences. We would naturally expect that such highly developed languages as Chinese, Burmese and Shan, would have contributed largely to the Kachin vocabulary. But such is not the case. The Jinghpaw dialect is remarkably pure, and has a vocabulary of at least fifteen thousand words, which is quite sufficient for all ordinary requirements. Very few Chinese terms have been incorporated, although the Kachins for centuries have been in close contact with their powerful and intelligent neighbours. It is almost exclusively the Gauris that have borrowed a few words, and in their pronunciation, especially in the gutterals, betray a Chinese influence. The Burmans have never exerted any marked leadership in any direction, and never came in friendly contact with the Kachins. They ruled the hills only nominally, and there was little intercourse between what was usually two hostile camps. Very few words have found their way from Burmese into Kachin. Since Kachin schools have been opened, and Burmese text-books are used, a few religious terms have gained admittance from this source, but it has been found that in most cases these can be replaced by pure Kachin words.

Shan has, however, contributed more both to vocabulary and general ways of thinking than either Chinese or Burmese. A glance at the dictionary will at once reveal the indebtedness of the Kachins to the Shans. A large number of words, expressions and idioms in constant use are taken from the Shan. They have through long usage been ingrafted into and become a part of the Kachin stock. It is also noticeable that while very few Kachins (apart from those that have attended school), speak the Burmese with any degree of fluency, most Kachin men of the Northern Shan States and also in other parts of Kachin-land speak Shan with ease. This is not because Shan is easier than Burmese or because the two dialects are particularly related. Burmese is philologically nearer Kachin than Shan and the tones present difficulties to the Kachin ear. But all the hill-tribes have had more to do with the Shans than with the Burmans, and it furnishes another illustration of how a conquered people with a higher form of civilization will in time put its mark on the conquerors.

Jinghpaw the leading dialect. Among the Kachin dialects the Jinghpaw is in every particular the leading form of speech. Atsis, Lăshis and Mărus as a rule speak Jinghpaw fluently, being troubled only in the pronunciation of certain words. The Atsis for example connot give the *r* sound but soften it down to *y*. But these peculiarities are of small importance. The fact that there is one leading dialect all over Kachin-land is an immense advantage to all. The Jinghpaw has for about twenty years been reduced to writing and has the beginning of a literature. It is not likely that any of the other dialects will be thus honored, and from an educational point of view it is not desirable or necessary. In time all will learn to read and write Jinghpaw, and the less important dialects will be relegated to obscurity and be eventually forgotten.

The Măru group. The Măru, and its daughters Atsi and Lăshi, have not sprung directly from the Jinghpaw, but come from the same source. The Măru may be spoken by about 25,000 or 30,000, and the Atsi by a few thousands more, while the Lashi represents a number smaller than the Mărus. But our information is very uncertain as to these particulars. We have already advanced the theory that the reason Jinghpaw has departed, at least in appearance, more widely from the original than the Măru, is because of its closer contact with the outward world. The Mărus and kindreds are lower in the scale of civilization, because of their more isolated life. Still, in saying this we wish again to remind the student that we are merely speaking from outward appearances. If ever an exhaustive study is made of these dialects we will probably be called upon to reverse some of our opinions regarding them. From such studies as I have been able to make, I am quite convinced that these dialects are not any more closely related to Burmese than is Jinghpaw.

Vocabulary. The "meagre" vocabulary of Kachin has often been a subject of remark. But the fact is that the meagreness has been with our knowledge rather than with the vocabulary. As already stated the language certainly has fifteen thousand words, and few men make use of such a word-list in English. Many of these words are obsolete, or nearly so, for every day use and have been relegated to the religious formulas known only to the old men, the priests and the professional story-tellers. But they are still recognized as a part of the language, and will again be found useful as the literary work advances and new ideas demand new terms. We may find it hard to explain how an illiterate mountain people could have retained so large a vocabulary, but we have other instances to show that backward races have had a much larger supply of both words and ideas than has generally been supposed.

Relations to other groups. Some of the philological questions raised by the study of these dialects are decidedly interesting. The relation between the Kachin and Naga dialects indicates a close affinity, and the same holds true of Kachin and the Chin group. The dialect of the Lăkai Chins to the north-west of the Hukong valley may be regarded as a branch of Kachin, but they call themselves Chins, (Hkang). The further south we go among the Chin tribes, the more marked become the dialectical differences, but similarity of both vocabulary and grammar, not to mention customs and religion, prove beyond a doubt their close relationship. They no doubt came from the same northern regions. The Kachins and Karens have always claimed relationship, and some of the Karen traditions clearly prove that on their way south they became familiar with the country around Bhamo. Their customs, traditions and religious ceremonies are to a large extent identical. But in language the Karen belongs to the Chinese rather than the Burman side of the family. Many of the roots are the same, but tones and grammatical constructions compel us to classify Karen with Shan and Chinese. A comprehensive study of the sixty or more different dialects of Yunnan and the large number in the Southern Shan

States and Karen-land has not been undertaken. Valuable vocabularies are found especially in the Upper Burma Gazetteer, but much remains to be done before we are able to assign each dialect to its proper group, family and class.

The Source. The close relationship between the Kachin and Burman group of dialects, suggests a common source and origin. The Kachin dialects have however, not grown out of Burmese. The question is where to look for the original mother-tongue. Burmese is not the daughter of either Tibetan or Chinese. It is the sister of both. The families of languages represented by the names, Chinese, Tibetan and Burmese are the descendants of some Mongolian mother-speech, probably long ago buried and forgotten. We can only hope that as we learn more of the civilization that once existed in Mongolia and adjacent countries some voice from the past will help us to a satisfactory solution of this obscure problem. In naming the class of language to which Burmese and Kachin belong I still prefer the name Turanian. The name Polytonic cannot be referred to all the groups and dialects involved as some of them have long ago ceased to be tonal. Turanian or "Mongolian" are names in which this large family of languages can be included. I venture to present a list of the leading families and groups, even though I am fully aware that it is far from exhaustive.

A Group of Maru villagers.

A group of Maru villagers.

Classification.

TURANIAN CLASS.

Family.	Group.		Remarks.
Tibetan	Tibetan, Magar, Murmi, Lepcha, etc.		
Chinese	Chinese	Cantonese, Hakka, Lishaw, Maitso, and some 40 different dialects.	In Western Yunnan are supposed to be found over sixty dialects.
	Shan	Ahom, Kamhti, Mongtsa, Shan or Tai, Siamese.	Northern and Southern Shan have many differences.
	Karen	Sgaw, Pwo, Brec, Karenni.	
	Mon Annam	Palaung, Talaing, Khamu.	Mosho, Wa, La, Hkun, Anka, Hkwe — Some of those dialects show a close relationship to Burmese, others to Shan.
Burman	Burman	Burmese, Kadu, Taungthu, Danu, Arakanese,	
	Kachin	Jinghpaw, Maru, Atsi, Lashi, Nung,	The Sasan or Hkauri need not be regarded as different dialects; they are practically Jinghpaw.
	Naga	Hpon (?), Ao, Lotha, Garu, Mikir,	
	Chin	Siyin, Haka, Saushi, Yawdwin, Lakai, Chinbok,	

CHAPTER III.

COUNTRY, VILLAGE AND HOME.

The ancestral home of the Kachins was, according to tradition, a high table-land far to the north. Their present territory is a wild mountain country intersected by narrow valleys and deep gorges, through which flow numerous mountain streams. These are all tributaries to the great rivers, the Irrawaddy and the Salween. The ranges run mostly north and south. They rise all the way from one thousand to seven or eight thousand feet above sea-level; but the average altitude is between four and five thousand. Peaks above eight thousand feet are few, and only one or two attain the height of ten or twelve thousand. Small valleys, that in former ages were the beds of mountain lakes, are quite numerous, but extensive plains are found only in the Irrawaddy basin and along its main tributaries. Of these the *Tănai hka* (the Chindwin), drains the Hukong valley, the largest low-land settlement among the Kachins. The Mogaung river flows partly through Kachin land, but its banks and plains are inhabited mostly by Shans and Burmans. The Taiping goes through the Gauri hills, emptying into lowlands occupied by Shans, Burmans and a few Chinese. Along the romantic Salween Kachins hold the west bank for a considerable stretch. On the east bank different kinds of Shans and Palaungs live among the high rugged hills. The picturesque and magnificent river with its superb and in many places unsurpassed scenery drains a comparatively narrow strip of territory, probably nowhere exceeding one hundred and fifty miles in width. This barrier is the natural boundary to the east, and the difficulty of fording the river even during the dry season probably had a great deal to do with the fact that few Kachins gained a foot-hold on its eastern bank. The great rivers are fed by hundreds of smaller streams, many of which, especially during the rains, become wild mountain torrents most dangerous to ford. Beautiful scenery is found everywhere. A few of the waterfalls can stand comparison with some of wider reputation. Of these we can mention only the Namhpa fall near Sinlum, east of Bhamo; the Gumlau fall north-east of Sima, and the Npa fall half way between Bhamo and Shwego.

Fauna. The animal life of the mountains in the whole of northern Burma is with only a few variations the same as that of the plains. Elephants and rhinoceros are not now found above the foot-hills, but tradition claims that both these pachyderms were once common at higher elevations, and some affirm that they are still to be seen in some of the dense jungles along the Salween. Herds of elephants are still found in the Hukong and many of the chiefs in the valley are in possession of valuable rhinoceros' horn testifying to the existence of the animal in that vicinity. The tiger and the leopard, with many smaller species of the *Felidæ,* are distressingly abundant, and in many localities on the increase, as the inhabitants have been practically disarmed. Wild dogs hunt in packs, but seldom trouble the villages. Smaller kinds of carnivora make the keeping of fowls and pigs an anxious problem. Bison is now and then seen in the hills, but is generally confined to the low-lands. Wild hogs, deer and monkeys give the cultivators a lively time, being with difficulty kept out of the fields. Squirrels, badgers, porcupines, weasels, rabbits and numerous species of rats present a variety for the curry pot. The pangolin or ant-eater is not unknown. Otter is found in almost any stream. Bears are in some localities as much feared as tigers and seem to be more often in evidence. Bats are numerous, especially in some of the caves which abound in the hillsides.

Of small birds the hills present a greater variety than the plains, and all furnish meat for the table. During the cool season nearly every Kachin carries his bow and clay-pellets for the shooting of small birds, but the destruction is not great. Pheasants, peacock, jungle-fowl, pigeons, quail, ducks and geese tempt the more ambitious hunter, but our Kachin is not a success for this kind of game. Birds of prey are a constant menace to the poultry, and necessitate eternal vigilance. Hawks of all kinds are constantly about, and now and then an eagle will carry off a small pig. The cuckoo and the lark remind the European of home. The cuckoo sings from the middle of March to the end of May. The song of the lark in the Northern Shan States is as clear and sweet as that of the European species. Other singing birds are quite numerous, and during the beautiful spring mornings the wooded hills are alive with song and songsters. The horn-bill is sacred to the Kachins. Cranes and herons visit the valleys, especially during the cool season. Woodpeckers and paroquets, often with gorgeous plumage, are always an interesting sight.

Among the reptiles the hamadryad is the most feared. A small viper called the *pu htum* figures in Kachin tradition as having caused the death of the "nine brothers" who indirectly caused the deluge. Not knowing which was head or tail they were all killed by the careless handling of the snake. The python is eaten, and "python-gall" is a very valuable medicine. Snakes are numerous, but poisonous varieties seem to be few. Of lizards there are various kinds, and the chameleon holds a prominent place as the "serpent" in the Kachin story of Eden.

Flora. The vegetation among the lower hills is semi-tropical; at higher altitudes we meet trees and flowers familiar to a temperate climate. The pine grows freely in certain parts of North Hsenwi. Species of oak and birch, and a number of trees with beautiful flowers, of which the *bauhinna* is the most noted, give the hillsides a rich and variegated appearance. Beautiful orchids, of which the *Dendrobium* family is the best known, have brought the hillmen many a rupee. It is to be regretted that the ignorant greed which has indiscriminately brought every plant, young and old, to the market, has practically exterminated the more valuable species within British Burma. Most of the orchids shipped from Bhamo, or coming by the way of Namhkam, have been collected within Chinese territory.

Rubber was formerly abundant in the Hukong, but the trees are rapidly being killed, as the Kachins extract every drop of sap that can be had from top to root. Of fruit trees we have the apple (a kind of crab), pear, plum, cherry, peach, quince, walnut and chestnut. But all the varieties, except the walnut, are of very inferior quality. The attempts that have been made to introduce European fruits have not been successful. The heavy rainfall is detrimental to the development of the trees. Raspberries and wild strawberries grow above an elevation of 2,500 feet. Home vegetables do well as a rule especially during the cool season. Maize and potatoes are cultivated more and more and with good success. As the climate is moderate the Kachin hills could without difficulty support a European population. The heat is not greater than in South Africa, or in the southern parts of the United States. The soil as a rule is rich, and with proper methods of cultivation would yield richer harvests than the crude ways of our hillmen make possible.

The Village. Formerly every village site was chosen with a view to protection from an attacking enemy. Tribal feuds and intestine warfare belonged to the order of the day, and it was necessary for the chief and his subjects to perch their homes in the most inaccessible places. The villages as a rule were large and far between. But this is rapidly being changed as a result of the peaceful life under the British administration. The once large villages are breaking up and small communities settle wherever it is most convenient. Many of the modern villages exhibit but few of the characteristics of the former life.

The typical Kachin village is approached by a long, wooded, often picturesque entrance called *măshang*. On each side of the road are placed a certain number of short, hewn or squared posts (*lăban*), covered with rude pictures of grain, weapons, household articles and ornaments. These are "prayer-posts." The figures represent such things as are most desired and valuable to the community, and as the providing "spirits" have their place just beyond, they are thus constantly reminded of the communal need and wishes. Having passed the prayer-posts, we find, usually under some tall and venerable trees, a number of altars, "shrines," and shelf-like structures, to which are tied innumerable bamboo sections wrapped up in large leaves. These things are sacred to the spirits (*nats*), the divinities worshipped by the chief as representative of the village. Conspicuous is, as a rule, an enclosure dedicated to the spirit of the earth, (*shădip*), where special offerings are made on important occasions. There are often stretched across the road bamboo splits tied together so as to make a long line, on which are hung numerous star-shaped bamboo ornaments. This is to keep off spirits that cause cholera, small-pox, cattle disease or the like. Larger communities usually build a small hut, or house without walls, in this place, in which annual harvest sacrifices are offered. Otherwise it is not used. In the "good old days" the village entrance was not only a place where religious ceremonies were performed, but often presented scenes of quite a different character. In case of a blood-feud, or if the payment of a debt had been unduly delayed, the aggrieved party would try to force a speedy settlement by taking possession of the "grove," and from there direct their operations towards the village. They might drive a certain number of pegs into the ground vowing to tie a cow or a pig from the offending village to each one before they left, if an agreement could not be reached. They would kill pigs and fowls and in every way harass the unfortunate village until their demands were granted. This interesting way of collecting a debt now belongs to the past within British territory.

Having passed the village entrance, there is usually a short distance before the village, or only some of the houses, suddenly emerges out of the jungle. A large village covers a considerable area, as the houses are built far apart for safety in case of fire. They are perched on narrow ridges, or hung on the steep hill-side with the jungle close at hand. The house of the chief (*htingnu*), as a rule occupies the most desirable locality and is the most typical, even though they are all built on the same pattern. In front of the "palace," and in fact before every other house, we notice a curious collection of shrines and altars similar to those passed at the entrance. These are altars and religious emblems dedicated to the household spirits, the supernatural guardians of the family. No one may interfere with these insignia of worship. They are all receptacles of the various kinds of offerings, and are kept intact to remind the spirits that they are constantly remembered. The initiated can easily tell to what kind of a spirit a certain altar is dedicated. There are usually two kinds representing the household *nats*, two for the celestial spirits, and one or more kind for the spirit of the earth. The high structures to the celestial spirits (*mu* and *sinlap*), are always conspicuous. A low altar, by the side of which is seen a tall bamboo pole from which are suspended rude representations of the sun and the crescent moon made of bamboo sheets, remind us that the "spirits" ruling these luminaries are here invoked. A large number of St. Andrew's crosses testify to the number of cattle that have in the course of time been sacrificed for the good of the family. If the community can boast of a "prophet" or medium (*myithoi*), a high scaffold-like structure ascended by a tall bamboo ladder will tell the tale. In this the "prophet" receives his inspiration and makes known the will of the supernatural agencies. Outside, or usually in front of the "palace," we as a rule notice a circular excavation. This is a dancing-floor,

Numshang or entrance to a village.

P. 40.

where a great religious dance is given whenever the chief feels called upon to give the entertainment, and is able to defray the expenses. In the Northern Shan States a a small shrine dedicated to a spirit called *Shăming* (Kachin *Jăhtung*), is often found near the village entrance. But this is an adaptation from the Shan and is never seen except where Shan influence is strong. (Comp. Chap. XIII; para. Nat-altars).

The home. Having passed the long lane which is a part of the village entrance and the place dedicated to the household nats, we enter the house of the chief. It may be longer and wider than those of his subjects, but plan, style and arrangement is the same in all. There is first a covered front without a floor where paddy is pounded, and where on a low platform towards the high side of the hill, wood, farming implements, baskets and the like are kept. Passing through this front there is the stable, covered and closely walled in, where cattle and horses are kept. After this cattle-pen or stable we reach the front steps, usually one or more notched posts, supported by a tall post the upper end of which is carved into the shape of a sword. We ascend to a narrow verandah about two or three feet wide, which serves as a roosting place for the fowls and a "store-room" where food is kept for the pigs. Pushing open the narrow, creaking door, we have on one side a long room for general use, and on the opposite the maidens' apartment (*nla dap*) where the young people can meet and amuse themselves. The Kachins hardly ever speak of rooms. The house is divided into certain number of "fire-places;" these may be walled off or not, but each represents an apartment or room. Groping our way through the darkness, as there are never any windows, we reach the men's "fire-place," where consultations are held and strangers are entertained. This is always situated on the side towards the rise of the hill, or else on the right, and opposite are the family apartments. These consist of a room for each married family, and one for the old people. Above the chief fire-place is the sacred corner, with a shelf-like "altar" dedicated to the family spirits. Tresspasses in this place are especially resented, and care should be taken not to touch or handle the religious emblems that may be close at hand. Passing the "spirit-place" (*nat ra*), we reach the back door which leads to a raised verandah and the back steps. There are never more than two regular doors, one at each end. In very long houses a low side-door may be found near the main fire-place, but this is not common. To have a long house is a sign of wealth and prosperity, and is a much coveted honor. Houses one hundred and fifty feet long are not uncommon, and some of the chiefs can boast a "palace" two hundred, or even two-hundred and fifty feet in length. Such a house is the home of a large number of families. Formerly each slave-family would have its own apartment, and then there would be a number of families belonging to the household. The space allotted to each was not large, but quite sufficient.

The houses are built on piles about three feet from the ground. The space below is walled in for the hogs and fowls. The Kachin dwelling is not as light and airy as the Shan and Burman, but much more substantial, and admirably adapted for a comparatively cool climate. During the day the people live and work out of doors, but at night several fires give heat and light. The smoke finds its way out anyway it can, and thus the whole inside becomes black and shining with soot. House-cleaning is practically unknown, and the bamboo floor allows dirt of all kind to fall down and accumulate below. When a dwelling gets too old, that is when it has stood seven or eight years, and has become too much inhabited for comfort, a simple remedy is to put fire to it and build a new one. If the head of the family dies, the widow and children will not as a rule consent to live in the house where he expired. It is either torn down or left to stand empty, and a new house is put up. Timber and bamboo are cheap and a house can be put up in a few days. Accidents by fire are not very common, but if a house does burn the loss as a rule is not very great.

A stranger must never enter a house for the first time by the back door. Both the first entrance and exit should be by the front door. Having once gone in and out through the main door he can come and go as he pleases, only he must always go out the same way he came in. If there is a fence around the house, clothing, saddles or the like must not be hung on it, nor must anything be placed along the eaves. Not to observe these and similar rules, the guardian spirits will be offended, and even though they may not do anything to the ignorant offender, they will surely punish the unfortunate inhabitants for allowing such impious liberties.

House-building is a communal affair, always in evidence during the cool season. It is made a time of festivity as well as of work. The owner will get out the timber, and when all is ready, the village people are called together by the beating of drums, gongs and cymbals. Men, women and children join in the work. The old men prepare bamboo splits for tying purposes, as no nails are used, The women cut and carry the thatch, and attend to the cooking department. The young men do all the heavy work and the children make themselves generally useful. The whole house may be put up in a single day, and it hardly ever takes more than two. But whether the house is finished or not, the "house-warning" (*ningshawn shang*), when the family and the guardian spirits take possession of the new dwelling, takes place, as a rule, on the evening of the first day. A priest recites his blessings, exhorting the spirits to fill the new place with prosperity and abundance. New fire obtained by rubbing two pieces of bamboo together is lighted at the principle fire-place. A generous feast is provided. A great deal of rice and curry, and above all, of native whisky is consumed. Laborers are not paid, but the "lord of the house" must supply all with food and drink.

Towards evening of a house-building day there is always an animated crowd, doing a great deal of talking and yelling, but very little work. All are more or less hilarious because of liberal imbibing. Quarrels, ending in a fight, are not uncommon on such occasions. But generally it is a good-natured crowd and the quarelling and screaming does not mean very much.

CHAPTER IV.

APPEARANCE AND DRESS.

The Kachins have been described as "very dirty with a repulsive type of countenance." That most of them are dirty, and some of them very much so, admits of no controversy, but their "type of countenance" is generally far from "repulsive." Washing is not a religious duty with most mountain people. Water has to be carried great distances often over steep mountain paths. During the dry season it is usually scarce, and must be used for more important purposes than bathing. In the cold weather there is small inducement to have a dip in a rushing mountain stream, as most Kachins declare it will give them fever, which is no doubt true. During the rains when they spend most of their time in the paddy-fields, where water is abundant, they often have a wash. When clean and properly dressed, both men and women compare quite favorably with either Shans or Burmans.

Physiognomy. It is difficult to say what is the general Kachin type, his particular cast and expression of countenance. All shades and types may be grouped together in the same community. The Mongol or Tartar origin cannot be doubted; but there has been a great deal of intermixture in days gone by, and climatic conditions have had their usual effect. Even among our rude Kachins blood will tell. The members of the ruling families are generally more refined and intelligent looking than those of the average "commoners," and their features are much more regular. It is quite easy to tell them in any gathering. Well to do families will allow a few extra luxuries, and being more in touch with the outside world, will betray refinement and "good breeding" above the ordinary.

Chiefs and other rich men formerly had among their wives Shan and Burman women, and the children of such unions would show their mixed parentage. The general type, however, is the short round face, low, often narrow forehead, high cheek-bones, oblique and widely separated dull eyes of the usual oriental complexion, broad nose, thick protruding lips and broad, square chin. The color of the skin may vary from almost negro black to the sallow tint of the northern Chinaman; but the ordinary shade is dark brownish. Many are found with complexion and features remarkably like the American Indians, while others might almost hail from southern Europe. This great diversity is best accounted for by intermarriages with neighbouring races, which formerly was much more common than now, and from climatic conditions.

The men, generally speaking, do not look strong or vigorous. Their average height is about five feet and four inches; but some measure close to six feet and present a fine physique. The women are somewhat smaller, but most of them are strongly built, and they are able to endure a great deal of hardship. The fact that the women work harder than the men has contributed to their physical development. Many of the men live a life of comparative idleness, spending their time in opium smoking, sleeping and drinking native liquor, complaining of all kinds of ailments. With care and proper habits the Kachins would be a strong race capable of a great deal of hard work and natural development.

Men's dress. Among the men there is no uniformity as to material worn, or the particular cut of coat and trousers. Nearly everything they wear is bought in the Shan, Chinese and Burman bazaars, and styles and shades vary accordingly. They buy whatever they can afford, which may mean an indigo colored suit worth a rupee and a half, or a cotton-padded Shan jacket representing a larger outlay. The Hkahku men have probably kept closest to the ancestral way of dressing. They wear a long, narrow, variegated turban, leaving the high top-not in view, a blue coat with long, wide sleeves, and a towel-like loin-cloth coming down to the knees. Among the southern Kachins, especially east of the Irrawaddy, the loin-cloth has given place to Shan or Chinese trousers. The turban, the pride of the men, varies according to means and surroundings. A long white turban worn in Chinese fashion is the rage among the Gauris, while south-east of Bhamo and near the Shan States they are all very partial to the silk head-wear of the Burmans.

Sword and bag. The only articles common to the men of to-day is the long, useful sword and the equally indispensible bag or haversack. No man is ever seen without these necessities. The true Kachin sword is now rarely seen south of Myitkyina and Mogaung. The Shan article is in common use. The bags are elaborately embroidered, and the different patterns indicate the taste and fancies of different communities. Thus we have the Hkahku, Gauri, Mǎru and Jinghpaw bags, each with peculiarities of its own. They often display a considerable amount of ornament, and young men carry a richly embroidered "towel" tied to the shoulder-strap, always the gift of some young women, and worn for her sake.

Women's dress. There is more uniformity among the women in regard to dress than among the men. They still make by hand nearly everything they wear. The only difference in style is such as is necessitated by climate. The women in the Hukong valley and generally on the west side of the Irrawaddy, wear a simpler and more comfortable dress than their sisters living at higher altitudes. The dress of the genuine hill woman is quite elaborate, picturesque and expensive. The married women put on a tall, folded *head-dress* of blue cloth; unmarried women and young girls go bare-headed, having their hair trimmed so as to hang down as "bangs," or in fringe-fashion. In the lobes of their ears they put long silver tubes with long fringes of red felt-cloth hanging down in front. In the

Amber-mines district the silver tube is replaced by long, candle-shaped pieces of clear amber of considerable value. From the upper portion of the ear, lappets or inlaid silver plates, fringed with embroidery and short tassels of beads, complete the head ornaments. Around the neck are hung several silver torques, and strings of amber, glass or porcelain beads. Beads, especially those made of petrified wood found in the amber district, are often family heirlooms highly prized. The wives and daughters of wealthy chiefs have a great deal of "jewelery" of this inartistic kind. Really valuable stones or gold and silver ornaments of an artistic nature are seldom seen. The *jackets* are short, with or without sleeves. The regulation jacket with long sleeves is generally elaborately decorated with embroidery, porcelain buttons, silver clasps and cloth of bright red or green. A row of silver discs or buttons go around the neck; a cross of porcelain buttons ornaments the back, and bands of red or green finish off the cuffs. The making of such a jacket requires some skill. The *skirt* is short, barely reaching below the knees. It is skillfully embroidered, many of the patterns being both artistic and effective. The Kachin woman is second to none in Burma when its comes to artistic weaving and embroidery. The skirt is put on so as to be folded at the right side, and is held in place by a large number of cane rings. The wearing of these rings, sometimes over a hundred, together with narrow bands covered with cowries, and lacquered bands of various designs, is peculiar to the Kachin women. The Palaung women put on a certain number of such rings, but not nearly as many as the Kachin. The Hkahku women and those that live on and near the plains, find such an abundance of finery too heavy and cumbersome, and prefer a few simple rings or a sash or a band. During the cold weather leggings are worn held on by a number of fine rattan rings. Some of the men put on Shan or Chinese shoes, but women never allow themselves such luxuries. Finger rings of silver are quite common, but gold is rare, and in many localities practically unknown.

The front of a house.

P. 48.

Those that live near the Shan bazaar may put on the heavy bracelets worn by the Shan women, or a cheaper kind made by the Chinese, but this is only for the more well to do.

A special holiday dress is not the fashion, but on great occasions, as when there is a dance (mănau), or at some specially important weddings, the more wealthy women and the young girls of the leading families will appear in beautifully embroidered skirts not otherwise worn; old men will turn out in long silk coats of Chinese pattern; but it is seldom an opportunity is given to see a crowd in such attire. Take it all through, the Kachins are well dressed when at their best.

Many of the men never change their garments. When a new coat or a new pair of trousers is needed, they are bought in the bazaar and put on then and there over the old, which will drop off by degrees. Children up to four or five years of age are scantily dressed. Many of them wear only a string around the waist, and another string serves as a necklace, from which is suspended several silver and copper coins, often to the value of several rupees. These are charms for protection or to insure good luck. A great deal of coined silver is plugged and wasted in this way. We would suggest that they use the money and buy clothing for the children, but to the Kachin this does not seem to be wise economy.

CHAPTER V.

CHARACTERISTICS, HABITS AND CUSTOMS.

Everyone acquainted with the hill tribes of upper Burma is impressed with the *independence* of the Kachins. This must not all be put down to ignorance or lack of refinement, even though they have no fixed form of salutation, and no words for "please" or "thank you." There are polite and impolite ways of speaking, but they do not approach the extremes of the Chinese, nor do they voice the humility of the Burmese. Even the most powerful chief is approached without the kneeling and cringing so marked among Shans and Burmans. There is a proper way to present a case, or introduce a conversation, and certain points of "etiquette" must be observed, but the chief is subject to the same rules when dealing with his people. This absence of formality, and this bearing of equality, is the natural result of a long life of freedom. They have never been slaves, and were never tributary to anyone. The Chinese and Burmans never in reality ruled the hills. The Kachin chief taxed the Burmans and Shans on the plains, imposed duty or blackmail on every trader or caravan that passed through his territory, and raided whenever he thought he had a cause or felt inclined. Without paying an annual tribute no Shan or Burman village could exist where the hillmen were within striking distance. The people along the large rivers would often sleep in boats when they had reason to fear a raid, and large communities like Bhamo and Sawadi were attacked and sacked more than once. Thus the Kachin regarded himself lord of all he surveyed, and held both Burmans and Shans in contempt. "You fire a prairie or kill a Shan just for the sake of doing it," is one of his proverbs that indicates his estimate of his neighbours. The chief, while nominally the head of the community, is very often a mere figure-head. One of the "elders," or someone more than ordinarily resourceful, is the real leader. Besides, any individual in trouble, if not satisfied with the decision of chief and elder, can always take the law into his own hands. If he and his party are strong enough they can dictate their own terms. A Kachin has a keen sense of his personal rights. He resents anything that interferes with his liberty, or what he regards as his due. He does not know how to take defeat gracefully, and never forgets or forgives an injury or wrong.

Revengeful. This characteristic is at the bottom of the large number of feuds which in former times kept families and communities in continual strife. Our Kachin is revengeful, but not cruel, and he ought not to be called treacherous. He is capable of fidelity and has his sense of honor. He regards it his duty to avenge every wrong done him or his family. In the case of a murder there is a blood-feud; if his women are wronged there is a fine to be exacted; if his cattle are hurt, or his fields are interfered with, there must be a reprisal or a settlement. If the offending party accepts the terms imposed, peace is declared and nothing more will be said or done. But if the opposite is the result there must be a fight to the finish. A feud for three, five or seven generations may be declared. A man may take a vow that he will not put on a turban until he has satisfied vengeance. In such cases children and grand-children must avenge their fathers. When a feud is on they are not particular as to methods, so long as they secure success. With them "all is fair in love and war," and if the enemy can be punished without loss to themselves so much the better. It is this trait that has given the Kachins the reputation of being treacherous.

A feud always becomes a family or tribal affair. All connected in any way whatsoever with the contending parties become involved. This has naturally led to strange miscarriage of justice, and from our point of view, cruel injustice more than once. When the Kachins first came in contact with Europeans, they found it difficult in criminal cases to understand our point of view. If one of their men had been killed or robbed, say in Bhamo, the whole city became involved, and the relatives would take vengeance on anyone coming from that community, even though the victim may never have heard of the case. Years may have elapsed and the deed forgotten by all except the avenging spirits, the relatives. There was of course a reason even for so arbitrary a law. They knew that if a man was killed in a place like Bhamo, there would not be one chance in a hundred that the murderer would be handed over to Kachin justice, and thus to teach a lesson the first individual from that community that happened along would have to pay the penalty. Some Chinamen from Bhamo were once killed by a Kachin chief, because of a murder committed years before by a Burman. A party of missionaries were attacked and robbed in the Gauri hills for some imagined wrong held to the account of a British expedition sent into Yunnan nearly twenty years before. If the British rule should be withdrawn it would be impossible for a white man or native of India to pass through the hills without serious trouble. They would remember all killed in a fight or imprisoned, and the first "foreigner" coming along would have to pay the "price of blood." The logic of this may not appeal to us, but it is not so very long ago since similar "laws" were enforced both in Europe and America.

Reserved. The numerous feuds, and the chance of always meeting an individual or party with which his family had an unsettled dispute, made a Kachin suspicious and reserved. They never gave correct information to strangers regarding their business and whereabouts. This trait often aroused comment, and our friends have been called "awful liars." They do not always tell the truth, but they are not habitual liars. It is again their point of view slightly different from ours. When a European asks a Kachin whom he meets on the road, "Where do you come from?" he is sure to get the correct information; but the same question by an unknown countryman would elicit an evasion. In the first case there would be no danger in telling the truth, in the second case their might be. When entering a village, if our first questions concern the number of houses or the amount of paddy harvested, even the most truth-loving Kachin will prevaricate. This is not because of his love of lying, but he cannot see why this should interest a stranger, or he may suspect that you are an official on inspection with a view to increased taxation. But when we really know the Kachin and have gained his confidence, we realize that he is an interesting individual, intensely human, in most particulars very much like ourselves, loving a good story and a good time and seeing the point of a joke as readily as anyone.

Honesty. Taken as a whole the Kachins are remarkably honest. There is little stealing among themselves. Kachin servants can, as a rule, be trusted. The thief in the olden time was either killed or sold as a slave. This had a most salutary effect, which unfortunately is beginning to wear away. In the matter of "owning up," a man put to the test may consult his convenience; but as a regular thing they will tell the truth, or you will know what is the truth if you know how to make due allowances and deductions.

Hospitality, Every stranger stopping over night in a Kachin village is sure of his food and lodging. The chief is in duty bound to entertain all visitors, or if he is not able to do it, one of the "elders" must do the honors. The guest receives it not as a favor, but as an established right. A visitor may stay a number of days and nothing is thought of it. As a rule, however, they do not impose on the host and take no undue liberties. The host is responsible for the good behaviour of a stranger as long as he remains, and must do his utmost to find and punish him in case he has committed an offense. To refuse entertainment (*mănam daw,*) would be regarded a grave insult and might lead to a feud.

Personal habits. Men, women and children *chew* betel-nut, tobacco, cutch, lime, and several kinds of narcotic leaves that they grow or pick in the jungle. It is a filthy habit, and it makes havoc with their teeth. The common excuse for chewing is that if they do not do it the "mouth will smell." All *drink* the native whiskey or beer and eat malted rice. Those that can afford it get the distilled liquor from the native bazaars. Ordinarily the people do not drink to excess. They call their "brew" by various poetic names, such as "heavenly sweat," or "milk from Chyănun" (the mother of all Kachins), and use it constantly. But it is only at the great festivals, at the time of house-building and when special sacrifices are offered, that moderation is discarded and drunken orgies are the rule. Inebriates and habitual drunkards are found, and during the cool season when a number of "feasts" call the crowds together a great deal of liquor is consumed; but during the rest of the year scarcity if nothing else keeps most of them sober. Practically all of the men and some of the womed *smoke* tobacco, which they raise themselves. In some localities the use of opium both for chewing and smoking is on the increase. This is greatly to be regretted. In the Northern Shan States the poppy is extensively cultivated, and the use of the drug is assuming alarming proportions. The result will be greater poverty than ever. A Kachin is always disinclined to work and relegates all the drudgery to the women. Once under the influence of opium he rapidly becomes a worthless and hopeless burden. His one aim in life will be to satisfy his depraved appetite, and to secure his opium he will do almost anything. Very few have moral strength enough to give up the habit once it has a hold on them. (Comp. Chap. VI. para. *Opium*).

Food. A Kachin is rather particular about his food. He can make a meal from almost anything that grows in the jungle, but is much more fastidious in regard to his flesh-pot. He never touches flesh of the *feline* family. Killing a tiger, he will smoke and dry the meat to sell it to the Burmans. They use it for medicine, and the Chinese utilize the bones for the same purpose. Dogs are eaten only by the Mărus, who are despised on account of it. The python is the only snake dished up for curry, and monkey is relished only in certain localities. Crows and hawks are seldom eaten, but nearly every other kind of bird is regarded as fit for food. Fish of every kind is accepted. Cattle that have died by disease are rarely eaten, nor is blood of killed animals used at all. In preparing and handling the food they are very careful. They never touch the boiled rice with their bare hands. They always use ladles or leaves singed and half dried when dishing up the meal. No one need hesitate to partake of a dish of Kachin rice.

There are a good many rules and superstitions as to food and drink. Some water or liquor is always poured on the ground as a libation to the "spirits" before drinking. Children must not eat eggs, or their feet will not grow. Honey or porcupine flesh must not be given to a pregnant woman, as it will cause miscarriage. Green pumpkins cause liver-trouble, no doubt true! Tiger's heart makes a man ferocious, and should be eaten during war time to arouse courage. Anyone eating pig's tail will be slow; eating food intended for a person who has just died will make one forgetful. If children eat the liver of the mole, they will be indifferent to parents and relatives. If a man eats crows he will be nervous and frightened; if he eats the wing of a fowl his skill will be onesided. Eating the meat from the head of a cow, misfortune in cattle-dealing will be the result. If women eat the entrails of fowls, their yarn will be snarled while weaving. These are only a few of the pleasantries along this line.

Customs. Social customs and rules of "etiquette" differ somewhat in different localities. Many of the Gauries have

Women in full dress.

P. 56.

adopted the Chinese way of bowing, and a few strongly influenced by Shans and Burmans will show courtesy in their peculiar ways; but these are exceptional cases, the true Kachin customs still being the standard. A Kachin will, to the general observer, look rude and unrefined, but he has his code of morals and conduct and rules of etiquette.

The acknowledged form of introduction and friendly interchange of courtesies is by exchanging betel-nut boxes. This being done conversation will flow freely. Absolute strangers are introduced by their family names, and they are asked to help themselves from the box or from a bamboo filled with liquor. In general conversation one rarely hears anything foul, smutty or objectionable. They are not ordinarily given to low talk. The language is rich in euphemisms and most delicate subjects can be discussed in a natural manner.

The family relations are all that we can expect. Infidelity within the married state is not common, and a divorce is next to impossible. (See the chapter on Marriage Ceremonies). The young people are, however, allowed too great freedom, and this has led to the worst side of their customs. But, as we will point out in a later chapter, we must not judge them entirely from our standards of morality. Wife-beating is allowed, but it is not common. Children grow up without much care, and the parents have very little control over them. Old age is highly respected, and the old people are well taken care of.

Many are quick-tempered, and "swearing" is quite common by both men and women. If anything goes wrong it is likely to bring an oath to their lips. The usual forms of imprecation are: "May the *nats* (spirits) bite you;" "May tigers maul you," "May lightning strike you," "May you die by accident," "May your women die in confinement." Foul terms of abuse are not lacking in a heated quarrel; but as a rule there is very little quarelling, and one seldom sees a fight among them, except when they are under the influence of liquor.

Some of the rules observed in "good society" are the following: Visitors, as has already been told, must always enter a house for the first time by the front door, and depart the same way. A man must never pass behind, but always in front of another; this because a man always carries a sword and may attack from behind. Women may pass behind a man, or if passing in front must bend low and gather their skirts so they do not touch anyone. On the road a woman must always carry a basket and follow behind the man. A gift must be presented and accepted by holding out both hands. To use only one indicates pride and disrespect. One must not eat in the presence of visitors or strangers without first asking their permission, nor must anyone leave a house or a place without first asking, "May I (or we) go"? The host or the party addressed will then say, "Go," and liberty is given to depart. There are quite a number of "farewell" expressions wishing one a happy journey, and those that depart express the hope that those remaining behind may have a pleasant time and be satisfied alone. No one may enter the family compartments in the house of a stranger without special permission. The host must offer visitors and guests the best the house can afford. Theirs is the place of honor at the chief fire-place, and they may be asked to regard the house as their own.

Meeting strangers on the road one must never ask, "Are you well?" (*Kăja nni?*) This form of salutation, which has become customary when Europeans address Kachins, implies acquaintance and familiarity, not tolerated except between friends and relatives. In the good old days a stranger unfamiliar with Kachin ways would be imprisoned and fined if using this form of salutation when meeting persons he had never seen before. It is perfectly proper to ask anyone on the road, "Who are you?" "Where do you come from?" "What do you carry?" "Where are you going?" or the like. Only after being properly introduced (*shăchyen*) is it permissible to enquire as to the health and welfare of the individual and his family. These rules are violated constantly by Europeans not familiar with the intricacies of Kachin ways and customs. The hillmen, however, take it good-naturedly, because they cannot do anything else, and most of them understand that the "bad form" of the white man is due to the fact that he does not know any better!

CHAPTER VI.

GOVERNMENT AND LAW.

The Kachin form of government comes in its conception nearest to the patriarchal, and in its everyday working to the communistic. Practically each village, large or small, has its own headman or chief, who with the help of the "elders" manages the affairs of the community. Here and there an unusually enterprising and aggressive chief may have under him subordinate chiefs or headmen, but this is the exception. Ordinarily each chief is quite independent in his village or community. The chief belongs to one of the five families of chieftains, (See Chap. I), and he gathers around him such representatives from the families of commoners as are drawn his way. These can always leave the village if there are greater inducements in different directions. The village and the inhabitants may, for the sake of convenience, be called by the family name of the chief, but there is no tribal or family relation between them. When we speak about a Măran or Lăhpai village, we have in mind a community ruled by a chief from one of these families; but his subjects may represent scores of ordinary families distributed all over the country. The name of the chief is nothing to them, their regular family name is what counts, especially in their marriage relations. Nowadays when land is all taken up and new conquest is impossible, there may be a number of chiefs in the same village; they may or may not share in the government. A chief can never in theory become a commoner, but in reality many of them have degenerated and lost their authority and even intermarried with families of the common people.

In the Hukong valley, and in some localities especially in northern Kachin land, a number of communities are ruled by "rebel" (*gumlau*) chiefs. They represent a movement of some forty years ago directed against the hereditary (*gumsa*) chiefs, with a view to enable any man who could secure a following to become leader, headman or chief. The organization of these democratic communities does not materially differ from the regular ancestral government. The rebel chief has theoretically no authority to offer to some of the great spirits, especially the *mădai,* and can thus never give a religious dance (*mănau*); but having usurped the power of the hereditary chief he may find some way, if so inclined, to exercise his privileges. This movement for independence is now at an end, as the British Government recognizes the hereditary chiefs. Our concern is also with the regular order of things as handed down from ancestral times.

The Chief. In every community the man of first importance is the chief (*du wa*). Not that he is always the ablest, strongest or most influential individual there; but he is always regarded as the representative of the village. It is a mistake, however, to call a Kachin chief a Sawbwa, a term introduced from the Shan. He is, with very few exceptions, nothing but a village headman with limited power. The youngest son becomes chief after his father, and takes over the old home. The older sons either seek a domain of their own, or remain in the village with the title of chief, but in most cases with none of its prerogatives. Nowadays there is nothing for them to do but to remain and make the best of it.

The authority of the chief, and his influence in the community, depends entirely on his strength of character and personal ability. If he is intelligent, aggressive and enterprising, his rule will be practically autocratic. If weak, easy-going and indifferent, some-one of the "elders" will be the real ruler, while he only carries the title. In days gone by many of the chiefs never worked, but led a lazy life, becoming slaves to whiskey, opium and other vices. These men and their descendants are today very often the poorest and weakest in the community; their old ways of livelihood have been taken away from them, and they have not been able to adjust themselves to the more exacting conditions.

Tribute to the chief consists in one or two baskets of paddy a year from each household; certain days of labor from the whole community at the time of planting and harvest, and a hind-quarter of every animal killed as a sacrifice or in hunting. Nowadays most chiefs find it difficult to collect this moderate amount, as the people are unwilling to pay taxes both to their own chiefs and to the British Government. But in the glorious days gone by the chief that could tax the lowlands and levy duty on passing caravans lived in abundance. They grew rich and important, could afford quite a harem where even Burman and Shan women would be found; they would have a large number of slaves, ponies and herds of cattle. Many had pretentious framed houses, often stockaded, built in Chinese style. The villages they "protected" on the plains brought them a handsome revenue, since protection always meant that no one should have a right to fleece them but they themselves. When all this was done away with by British rule, no wonder the chief all of a sudden discovered that he was the most destitute man in the village. Many of them had few fields to fall back upon; their herds were soon depleted by the constant sacrifices; their slaves ran away; caravans could pass by their door without paying as much as a handful of salt; Shans and Burmans, and even their own people paid no attention to them any more. It was a most radical change and the memory of it still lingers. It is hard for the old chiefs to forget and forgive; they long for the day when the "Kala" will depart and the ancestral glory be restored. We cannot blame them for feeling as they do; it is human nature, and there is a great deal of this in the Kachin breast.

The Village Pleader. In some of the larger villages a man of influence, called the *bawmung*, (a Shan word meaning the "father of the country"), is the real ruler. He is a kind of "pleader," and is always a man of strong character and personal force. In a community where this official is found the chief has usually very little to say. The *bawmung* is always a man of the people, and holds his position solely because of superior ability, and what he decides is generally accepted.

Elders. Most communities have no *bawmung*, but there are always two or more elders, "aldermen," (*sălang*), whom the chief consults in all cases of importance. One of these is recognized as the "big elder;" he is one of the oldest and most experienced men in the community, and what he and his associates decree generally becomes law. Only an exceptionally strong chief would ever dare to oppose the elders. In all matters of special importance or gravity a council of the elders is called. Recognized leaders from outside communities may also be consulted. This council (*salang bawng*) is the Kachin highest court of justice, and decisions there reached are final.

Religious Officials. The men attending to the religious side of the community may or may not be directly concerned with its civil affairs. They are ordinarily men of great influence and leadership. The priest must be consulted in every undertaking of any importance, and often he serves as an elder. Still, their work must be viewed from the religious side and properly belongs to the chapter on religion and worship. (Comp. Chap. XIII; para. *Priesthood*).

Property. All the land within the circle of the chief nominally belongs to him. No outsider can settle down in his village or obtain land without his permission. All highland fields are allotted by him and personal ownership is recognized only as long as they are cultivated. When left, or allowed to grow up again into jungle, they again become common property subject to the will of the chief. This is almost ideal socialism. Lowland fields, requiring more labor and care, belong, however, to the family that first opened and cultivated them. They are handed down

Women carrying baskets.

P. 64.

from father to son. But they cannot be sold without the consent of the chief, nor can they be bought and become the property of a man living in another community. All the jungle surrounding the village is common property. Anyone can take all the wood and timber he needs. Bamboo planted and fenced in, as well as fruit trees, are regarded as personal property. Still there is nothing wrong if passers by help themselves. Things grown within a garden must be respected, but the rules are not nearly as strict as in higher forms of civilization. The chief can allot land to his subjects, but he cannot refuse anyone a field or a garden. He cannot act arbitrarily in these matters, as he is likely to be censured by the whole community, and the injured party may declare a "grievance" resulting in a feud and an appeal to arms.

Law. Custom and precedent as handed down by tradition and interpreted by the chief and village council comprises the recognized law. Each case is decided on its own merits, but there are recognized rules to follow, and a generally accepted scale of punishments or compensation. The old Mosaic code of a tooth for a tooth and an eye for an eye does not satisfy the Kachin sense of justice. He demands at least double for the harm done, and in most cases five teeth for one. The general tendency is to squeeze out of the offending party all that is possible. If the accused is satisfied, or regards it useless to resist, the terms imposed are accepted and peace is declared. But if he and his party, which usually means his family, fieel strong enough to refuse, there is likely to be a standing grievance, or as it is expressed, a "debt," which may lead to a feud. It is in the settlement of these debts that the legal ingenuity is exercised, and from which a Kachin gets more excitement and enjoyment than from anything else. The ordinary cases that come up for settlement are:

Theft, (*lăgu hka*). It is customary to fine a thief double the value of the goods stolen. If he has robbed a chief he may be fined five-fold. Anyone assisting a thief, giving

5

food and shelter or concealing stolen goods has also a "debt" (*shat jaw hka*) to pay. In addition to the regular fine, cattle or hogs for sacrificing to the offended spirits must be paid. If the offender is poor and has nothing to pay, he may be expelled from the village, sold as a slave, or even killed. False charges for the sake of extortion are treated very much as theft, and this "debt" (*jăwat hka*), may lead to serious trouble. A Kachin is very sensitive and anything like an insult, a false charge or insinuation, is deeply resented, and may easily lead to a prolonged quarrel ending in bloodshed.

A Loan, (*hkoi shap hka*). This is a very general and hence not a serious offence, but decidedly difficult in settling. A Kachin borrowing money or grain never thinks of the day of payment. He regards it rather as a gift than as a loan. He hates more than anything else to pay taxes, a fine or a debt, and loves above everything else to get something for nothing. To collect an old debt is an art that only a few understand. It takes an immense amount of talking, and incidentally a great deal of time, food and liquor is consumed. But time is nothing to our friend, and if he can get his board while talking a week or two about a two rupee debt, he feels satisfied even if he does not succeed in collecting the amount. He can come again the next year and go through the same performance. The debtor is equally satisfied if there is another delay, furnishing one more chance not to pay at all.

Adultery, (*num shaw*). This is a serious, but not very common offence. The man is always held guilty, and under the ancestral law was killed, unless he was able to pay a very heavy fine. Nowadays a fine, half that in case of murder, is exacted. It is no use for the man to plead that the woman made the first advances or was a willing party. The "elders" will sum up the case in accordance with the well known proverb, "If a Shan is at fault he must die; in a dispute with a Kachin he must die; if heaven is at fault the earth is drenched, if the earth is at fault it deserves to be drenched." This means that in any case the man must pay the penalty. Rape on an unmarried woman would be settled by a fine; on a married woman death, slavery or a very heavy fine used to be the punishment. When a fine was sufficient, a bullock, a gong, a sword, and almost anything else that could be exacted, would be demanded. Nowadays cases of this kind usually come before the British court within administered territory.

Illegitimate children, (*sumarai hka*). A fine is always imposed on the father of a child born out of wedlock, varying according to the ability of the family to pay. It is not a serious matter, and on account of the great freedom allowed the young people offences of this kind are extremely common. The girl's family are to some extent disgraced, and it means to them a financial loss, as an *n-gyi kănu* (the mother of a bastard) has not the same chance in marriage as one with a more respectable record. The birth of the child takes place in the home of the man, but he must appease the spirits of the offended family. In some localities a special fine is exacted if the girl dies in confinement, but this is not an ordinary custom. The usual articles, cattle, swords, gongs, fowls, etc., are offered in compensation. The man is under no obligation to marry the girl, and generally does not. As long as he has paid the fine nothing more is thought of it.

Blood-money, (*bunglat hka*). Blood-money is demanded in case of murder (*si bunglat*), when an employee is hurt (*hkăla bunglat*) or killed (*lăsa bunglat*), and, in some localities, when an unmarried woman dies in confinement giving birth to an illegitimate child (*ndaug bunglat*). Murder is the most serious of all offences and the ancestral law was usually a life for a life. Gradually custom has established a more practical way, and if the offender was able and willing to pay, the case could be settled without further bloodshed. But the demands were always heavy and often far beyond the means of the murderer and his family. There might be requested, cowries or small silver ornaments for each of the teeth and nails of the murdered person; swords or spears for the fingers; guns for the arms; slaves or beasts of burden for the legs; expensive gongs for the head; jars or pots for the abdomen; besides cattle for sacrificing to the "fates;" and money to all particularly concerned. Such a fine would amount to Rs. 300 or more, and most families were never able to pay even if they promised to do so. Hence there would arise a blood-feud carried on generation after generation until vengeance was satisfied. But the greatest number of feuds originated with the offending party refusing to consider terms of settlement. In that case it became a matter of honor for the aggrieved family to execute vengance, and wipe out the disgrace and dishonor to the family name.

When a man has been hurt or killed while working for another, the employer's liability is recognized. A fine will be fixed according to the nature of the case. If killed, say, when clearing jungle or at housebuilding, the terms are decided by the village council. It is never regarded as murder or culpable homicide, but simply as an accident, and the fine is light. If a man has been killed when on a trading expedition for another, the employer is liable to a fine, or he must find and punish the murderer, turning over the amount received to the deceased man's family. If he is unable to do either of these things, he may authorize the relatives to execute vengeance at his expense. If an employee dies a natural death, the employer pays only a bullock for the funeral (*jăhpu nga*), a gong for the death dance (*kăbung bau*), and a skirt or a piece of cloth for the final ceremonies (*măjip nba*).

Desertion and Elopement. If a man puts away his wife he forfeits all he paid for her as a bride, and in addition must pay the disgraced family a slave, a buffalo, a gong and a sword, or a fixed sum of money. If a wife, without good cause, runs away and returns home, her parents must send her back to her husband. If they allow her to remain they must return the price paid for her with interest, or a sister must take her place. If the parents do their utmost to send her back, but she refuses for some good and acknowledged reason, such as cruelty or neglect, there is no blame on the parents and they do not refund the "price."

Elopement of unmarried people is very common, and comes under the general rules related to marriage customs; (See Chap. IV.) This is not a serious matter and is settled without much difficulty. Elopement with a married woman is regarded as adultery and is treated accordingly.

Inheritance. The youngest son (*uma,* of a chief, *hpung-dim,* of a commoner) remains in the old home and follows in the succession of his father. The older sons receive a share each of all portable property, and can remain in the village or move away, as they like. If the husband dies leaving grown children, the widow may go and live with one of her sons or else she is taken over by one of her husband's brothers, who then becomes responsible for the family. Inheritance never goes to the female side of the family. All disputes in regard to inheritance are taken up and adjudicated by the village council.

General remarks. As a rule the decisions of the chief and his advisers are just and equitable. Bribery is next to impossible except in cases where a chief, pleader, or elder is all powerful; but in the average community all are on an almost equal standing, and to bribe a whole council could not be done without detection. Moreover, the parties concerned need not abide by the verdict if they consider it unjust. They can always appeal to the public, and if they can secure a following they can force a reconsideration of the whole case. This is often done.

But in the last analysis the only recognized right is might. If the defendent and his party consider themselves strong enough to "fight it out," they will do so and it becomes a question of who can hold out the longest. Thus in the glorious days of old, which a Kachin, like most other people, regards as the golden age, there was often war to the knife and the knife to the hilt. Feuds innumerable are still on the list, and if the British power permitted there would be the same kind of fighting within a very short time.

No case of importance is ever settled without a sacrifice. The contending parties eat and drink together, dip their swords in the blood, and take an oath that there is eternal peace between them. The losing side always pays for the feast, and there is a special bullock sacrificed by the winning side (*pădang nga*), to announce the joyous fact that they have been victorious.

CHAPTER VII.
INDUSTRIES.

Kachin industries are extremely few and of a most primitive character. The whole population, from the chief down, are practically tillers of the soil, and even in this they show no particular skill, and their implements are the most crude and simple. The fields are generally small, and most of the work is done by the women. Few raise enough grain to keep them supplied for the whole year.

Slavery. Formerly slavery was very common, and the chiefs and the well-to-do had numerous slaves who did most of their work. But the slave market has been closed within administered territory, and slave labor there belongs to the past. Prisoners of war, "witches," impecunious and undesirable individuals and families, would be sold or disposed of as slaves. Shans, Burmans and Chinamen would be found among their number. Today it is only in the Hukong valley, and among the Kachins in Chinese territory that slavery is practiced on an extensive scale. In the Hukong may still be seen representatives of the races just mentioned, and also a few from the Assamese tea-gardens, kidnapped by Nagas and Chins and sold to the wealthy slave owners in the rich valley. In that district there seems to be no particular disgrace in being a slave, and no attempt is made to conceal the fact. But in other parts of Kachinland every one resents being called a slave. Ordinarily the bondmen were well treated; in fact they were regarded, and looked upon themselves, as a part of the family. A male slave could marry a free woman, but the children became slaves. The owner could sell or give them away, but they were seldom disposed of except when exchanged in connection with a marriage. The price paid for a bride included a slave, and her parents gave one as a part of the dowry. Refractory slaves would be beaten, put in stocks, or as a last resort, sold. The worst would be sold to the Chins who sometimes bought them for their annual sacrifices. The most effective threat to an unruly slave was this, "Do you wish to go to Chinland?" which implied that unless he behaved he might become a sacrifice to the Chin divinities. A slave could always be redeemed. A usual method when prisoners of war had been enslaved, was for relatives or friends to capture some from the owner's side and thus force an exchange. It will not be long before slavery will be extinct in all parts of Kachinland.

Agriculture. Farming in the hills consists mainly in the wasteful and destructive forest denuding process of jungle clearing. A piece of jungle is selected and all the vegetation on the same is cut down in February and March, and is allowed to dry to the end of April or middle part of May. Then there is a tremendous blaze on the hill-side and only the black stumps and a few big trees remain. The ashes fertilize the ground and a good crop is generally secured the first year. Less is expected the second year, and it is seldom that a field is cultivated three seasons in succession. After the second crop has been harvested the jungle is allowed to grow up again and no clearing is attempted for seven or eight years. But even with so long a period of rest the land gets impoverished and the jungle growth becomes less rapid. After a period of rotation of this kind nothing will grow but thatch, and the jungle fires sweeping over year by year will destroy all other plants and struggling vegetation. On such land rice cultivation is impossible. A certain amount of prairie cultivation (*hkai bang*) is attempted along the foothills, but it is a very uncertain crop and is often a failure. Large tracts of forest land have, unfortunately, already been denuded, and it is only a question of time when the whole hill-country will be bare, unless the Government interferes. Before sowing, the land is worked in a crude way with hoes, but nothing like

A bamboo raft with men from the north. P. 72.

plowing is attempted. The sowing is done in the most primitive way. The sower scratches the ground with a dibble while he drops in the grain as he walks along. The weeding of the fields occupies most of the rainy season and is mostly done by women and children. Harvest comes towards the end of October, threshing in November, and the carrying home of the paddy is usually finished about the middle of December. Threshing is done by the methods employed in Egypt and Palestine in the days of Abraham. The threshing floor is in the open, baffaloes tramp out the grain and the winnowing is by the hand-shovel. The straw is accounted of no value and is burned. In highland (*yi*) cultivation, hardly any rice is raised for the market. In fact, there is seldom enough for home consumption. During every rainy season many subsist on Indian corn, millet, and whatever they can pick in the jungle.

Lowland (*hkauna*) cultivation, following the methods of Shans and Chinese, is practiced mainly by the population inhabiting the Hukong valley, the Northern Shan States and the Gauri hills. Those who possess a certain amount of valley cultivation are usually well off. There is still a great deal of land that can be thus cultivated, and by scarping the hillsides into terraces, utilizing the numerous mountain streams, there would be a great addition of very productive paddy-land. This form of cultivation ought from an economic point of vew to be especially encouraged by the Government. In some parts of the hills, land formerly thus cultivated has been allowed to grow up again into jungle, on the plea that they have no buffaloes with which to work the fields. Cattle disease and above all numerous sacrifices to the spirits are responsible for this state of things. It would be a blessing to the people if the Government were to prohibit all sacrificing of cattle, even if it should interfere with their religious liberties. They would be better fed on account of it.

In addition to raising paddy, most villagers plant some maize, millet, tobacco, beans and sessamum. Pumpkins and cucumbers are grown with the maize. In small gardens they grow mustard leaves, yams and other kinds of vegetables for the curry. In some localities cotton, indigo, tea and sugar-cane are cultivated on a small scale. Some potatoes are raised, usually of a poor quality. But these things are considered side issues, to fall back upon when the rice crop has been a failure.

Opium. It is only quite recently that poppy cultivation has found its way from China into Kachinland. In the early experiment with the plant it was confined to small enclosures near the houses. During recent years large tracts of land have been put under cultivation, and this is still on the increase. In North Hsenwi and in other localities along the Chinese frontier the Kachins aim to supply the Chinese market in western Yunnan, as the plant has been prohibited in China. The use of opium both for smoking and eating is alarmingly on the increase, to the detriment of everything else. Even the rice fields are being neglected, as opium brings in ready cash, which again is squandered on the drug and in other ways. There can be no doubt that the opium habit has a great deal to do with the increasing poverty and moral and physical deterioration of the Kachins. The working of the poppy field is carried on in Chinese fashion. The ground is carefully worked. When the poppy head reaches a certain size a slit is made into it with a thin blade and the exuding sap, when dried, is gathered on a metal scraper. The raw product is sold to the Chinese or kept for home consumption. Many Kachins smoke the drug mixed with shredded and dried plantain leaves. The opium is liquified on a small copper dish, and the leaves are saturated with the drug. Then it is smoked in an ordinary pipe, a small pinch at a time. But this way of indulging is getting too tame for most consumers. They prefer the Chinese method, and the eating of the drug is on the increase. In some northern sections both men and women smoke, but generally the women are not subject to the habit.

Trading. A Kachin is not a trader like a Shan or a Chinaman. Natural inclination, distrust and illiteracy stand in his way. Even in localities where they are regular visitors to the Shan bazaars, they will attempt hardly anything more than the making of a few annas by selling garden stuff, native beer and some opium. They can hardly ever bring fowls or pigs to the market, as they must be kept for sacrificial purposes. A few will engage in caravan trading, the stock in trade being salt, dried fish and tea which they buy from the Palaungs. Of the conservation of natural resources they have no idea. Rubber, lac and orchids used to be indigenous to almost every part of the country. But the rubber trade, even in the Hukong, will soon be at an end because of the reckless way of tapping the trees. In a similar way the marketable orchids have also been exterminated, and are today found mostly across the Chinese frontier. Each man thinks that he better get out of it all he can; if he does not, someone else will. There is no thought of tomorrow. As a trader our friend is a failure. He cannot compete with Shans and Burmans, and if he makes a venture he is likely to lose his capital. He consequently finds it safer to shun speculation and high finance, and conceal his silver in some safe place in the jungle or under the house. Any other bank he is not inclined to trust.

Mining. Gold, silver, copper, iron, lead, amber, jade and marble, are found within Kachin territory. The famous amber mines in the Hukong district are owned by Kachin chiefs, but most of the work is done by adventurers from Assam and China. The amber is of good quality, and was formerly found in large quantities; but the output is growing less year by year. The rich, and by the Chinese so highly valued, jade mines north-east of Kamaing, also belong to Kachin chiefs. All the heavy and dangerous work in extracting the stone from the deep, hot mines is done by Kachin coolies; but the trade is controlled by Chinese and Burmese speculators. The population of the district does not particularly profit from the wealth of their country, and seem to be more than ordinarily ignorant and superstitious.

Some gold-washing is done north of Myitkyina, in the Hukong valley, and in the Northern Shan States. Gold-bearing streams are found nearly everywhere. The gold is of good quality, but comes in small quantities. North of the confluence there must be a considerable supply of gold, judging from the amount dredged and washed in the Irrawaddy. The story is that the natives are afraid of arousing the gold-thirst of the white man, and thus conceal the place and bring only a moderate amount to the market. Silver, copper and lead are found in various localities, but the pits or mines are not worked. The Chinese were formerly prospecting throughout this whole territory, and worked in many places where there is now nothing but dense jungle. The Kachins have no idea of how to melt and work the ore, and the mineral resources, which are no doubt considerable, remain to be developed.

Blacksmithing. Although every hill-man carries a sword (the Burman *dah*), and stands in need of a hoe and dibble, if not a plough-share, for his rice cultivation, a Kachin blacksmith is a novelty. All his hardware comes from the Chinese or Shans, except that some of the Hkahkus make, what may be called, the genuine Kachin blades. These are about eighteen inches long, broadening from the handle outward. They are never pointed, as is the Shan *dah*. There are at least four varieties, of which one with clear, wavy streaks of steel running down the blade, is the most valuable and appreciated. This sword was carried especially by chiefs and persons of importance. They are now hardly ever seen south of Myitkyina and Mogaung, while only a few years ago they were not uncommon south of Bhamo. The Shan product is cheaper, if not so durable, and the Hkahkus do not come south, as they formerly did, to dispose of their wares.

Hunting and fishing. Our hill-man is not a sportsman.

Kachins from beyond the confluence.

P. 76.

He is not an enthusiastic hunter; but with a good gun in his hands he will soon find the sport interesting. During the cool season, deer-hunting is engaged in, all the men of the community turning out to drive the game from its shelter into some open place where it is shot or speared. This is done for the sake of food, and all that have had a part in the chase receive a share. Trapping and snaring are also known and pitfalls are dug for large game. Traps and snares are set mostly for birds, and birdlime is also used. Tigers and other large game are rarely hunted unless it is a question of turning out after a man-eater or rogue elephant. Very few good guns are found in administred territory, and the stalking of dangerous game is left wisely alone. Their swords, spears, bows and arrows are not looked upon with the same confidence as when they knew of no other weapons. Most of the guns are only old flint-locks, worn out and uncertain; and those fired with percussion caps are only a shade better. Now and then a good gun is seen, and some of the chiefs have breech-loaders given them as presents from the Government; but they find it difficult and expensive to procure ammunition, and the guns rust away in some corner of the house.

Naturally the Kachins know little about fishing. In the deep pools of the swift mountain streams fish are always plentiful, but they have no means of catching them. The weighted hand-net, used by the Burmans in shallow water, is unsuited for mountain streams, and any other kind of net they do not know. Fishing baskets are used to some extent, and a poisonous creeper, which they pound into pulp, is employed in smaller streams. Pouring the liquid pulp into the stream the fish are stupefied and come to the surface. But the ordinary way of fishing in small streams is to divert a part of the channel leaving the bed dry. Whatever is stranded on the pebbles, or is fished out of the mud, goes into the basket. It is mostly crabs, snails, mudfish of various kinds (eel in particular), and small stone-suckers that make up the catch.

Weaving. The Kachin women are skilled in weaving and embroidery; but their methods and implements are most primative. They go through all the processes from spinning the cotton with a hand spindle to turning out the finished article. They know how to weave a number of patterns, some of them very effective, all of them exhibiting both skill, taste and patience. A weaving frame, such as the Burman and Shan women use, is unknown. The warp is held tight by means of two bars; the back bar is held in place by pegs driven into the ground, and to the front one is attached a broad leather belt which passes around the weaver's back. The operator sits on the ground or on a piece of board, her feet braced against a stout piece of wood or bamboo. Instead of working the heddles with her feet, she lifts them up with her hands, as she sends the shuttle back and forth. It is a slow, tiresome process, and weeks will be required for the finishing of a single skirt. It is all done out of doors, and it keeps the women busy from the middle of December to the end of March. There are a few accepted and generally recognized patterns and designs, but there is plenty of room for individual fancy, taste and skill. Some of the patterns for the bags, all of them woven, are really remarkable, and their work along this line, as well as in their hand embroidery, is always highly appreciated by Europeans.

The activity of the Kachin man does not arouse our admiration; they never hurt themselves by overwork, but see to it that the women are fully occupied and do not spend their time in leisure. It is hard to imagine a harder worker than a Kachin women. She costs her liege lord a neat sum when he marries her, and he regards it his right to take it out of her in labor. Before it is light she must be up and pound the paddy for the day. A visitor to a mountain village will never forget the peculiar sing-song grunts, groans and high-pitched tones that break the stillness of the early morning hour as the young girls begin the operation of pounding, husking and winnowing the paddy. A large wooden mortar and a heavy pestle are used to remove the husk, and the winnowing is done with a large, round wicker tray. It is a most exacting and fatiguing work. In many localities this back-breaking toil could be eliminated by utilizing water power, but the Kachin never imitates the skill of the Shans and the Palaungs in this particular. Having finished the paddy pounding then comes the carrying of water and the preparing of the morning meal, feeding the pigs and getting ready for the day's work in the field or at weaving. Water is often carried for nearly a quarter of a mile up steep hill-sides. Long bamboo tubes are used instead of buckets; these are placed in wicker baskets, carried on the back, the strap going across the top of the head. It is remarkable what loads these women can carry. In a few villages there is a rude attempt to lead a mountain stream; but usually such a labor-saving device is not considered. Springs in deep ravines are preferred. This is no doubt an advantage for the securing of good, wholesome water, but it means many weary hours for the hard working women. The picking, carrying and cutting of the wood is also her work, and it takes a good deal of her time. The wood is usually found in old paddy fields and is carried great distances. It is no uncommon thing to see a woman with her baby carried in front, a heavy load of wood or a basket of rice on her back, twirling a hand-spindle (*hkăbang*) as she trudges up the steep mountain path. Besides, she does her share of the work in the paddy field, sowing, planting or weeding. That she has no time for her home and children is not a surprise. In fact there is no word for home, and children run wild from the time they can walk till they are big enough for work.

It is no doubt the hard life of the women that is responsible for the large infant mortality in Kachin communities. It is no uncommon thing to find families that have had seven, eight, nine or more children of which only two or three have grown up to maturity. Families with no children, or where they have all died are often found. Deaf and dumb, blind, deformed and half-witted children are seen in almost every community. The hard life of the mother, and the free, unrestrained life before marriage, is no doubt largely to blame for these unfortunate conditions.

Baskets and mats. In common with all eastern peoples a mat is about all a Kachin uses for his bed, and a basket becomes an indispensible necessity in his daily life. He is somewhat skilled in basket weaving, but his mats are not equal to the products of Chinese or Burmese. Of baskets he weaves several kinds, of which we will mention three as particularily worthy of notice. First the wicker basket (*ka*) with no ornaments and put together in a simple manner. This is used for carrying wood and anything else of a general nature; bamboo tubes filled with water are also carried in this particular pattern. When on the road men always carry baskets of this kind. Women use them only for wood, water and work around the house. The regular woman's basket (*skingnoi*), is a neat and well woven article useful in endless ways. A woman is hardly ever seen on the road without this basket on her back carried by a brow band. Paddy is always carried home from the fields in these baskets, and all the woman's belongings find a place in its capacious hold. A basket very well made and rather expensive, called a "box" (*sumpu*), is used as we would use a trunk or a chest of drawers. It is never carried outside the house except when moving from one place to another. It has a close-fitting cover, and serves the purpose of a box quite well. Northern Kachins use a covered basket, with a curved top and a "trap door" (*sawng-hpai*), resembling when carried the coracle of an Irish fisherman. It is a most useful article as it is quite waterproof and easy to carry. In their basket making very little is done for the market. Most men know how to supply their own need, but they attempt very little more. Once in a while an old man makes basket weaving his particular work, and then confines his work to making

Ginning cotton.

Women weaving.

P. 80.

of the woman's basket (*shingnoi*), and of the kind called *sumpu*.

Mats are used in various ways, but so far as they are made by the Kachins they are all of the cheap, ordinary kind made of bamboo splits. The weaving of mats is not as much an art with them as is basket weaving. Those who can afford it usually buy the mats for sleeping and bed in the Shan or Burman bazaars. The poorer people have to get along with articles of their own manufacture.

CHAPTER VIII.

WEAPONS AND WARFARE.

Kachin weapons are guns, cross-bow, spear and sword. The sword has already been described (see Chap. VII.) The spears are of different makes and shapes. The regular Kachin *spear* is an unornamented point of steel with a shaft five or six feet long. But spears of Chinese or Shan make are frequently found. Some of these have double-edged spear-heads, and some are single-edged. The heavy Chin spear with its elaborate design of yak's hair is greatly valued and most of the chiefs have several of them. In days gone by a Kachin when travelling generally carried his spear as well as his sword, but nowadays the former weapon is seldom seen.

The *cross-bow* in the hands of a good "archer" or "shot" is an effective weapon. It is from three to five feet in span, and it is difficult for one not used to it to bend the bow. The arrows are made of bamboo, sometimes hardened in fire; stone or metal tips are not used nowadays, but formerly were not unknown. The Yawyins and the Lăshis very often poison their arrows with a kind of strychnine obtained from the nightshade, but the Jinghpaws seldom follow this practice.

Of *guns* several kinds are known and used. The most common are the "cheek-gun" (*săhkun sănat*), the flint-lock (*myiba*), and the cap-gun (*htunghpau*). The first may be called the real Kachin gun, and is by far the most common. It is a match-lock of Chinese and Shan make, fired with hemp fuse soaked in saltpetre. The gun is very light, with no butt and a very short revolver-shaped gunstock which is held in the hand and pressed to the cheek. The barrel is thin, and in most of the guns seen today with a ragged muzzle. In a few years more these weapons will be a novelty, as new ones are never seen, and the making of them has apparently ceased. Old flint-locks of various makes are met with everywhere. They have found their way into Kachinland from China, Assam or lower Burma. The cap-guns are more highly valued than any others, but the Government Arms Act makes it difficult to procure ammunition. A few chiefs have jingal and swivel guns, but they are becoming very rare. They belong more to the Shans than to the Kachins.

The Kachins know how to "pound" *powder.* Sulphur can be bought in any Shan bazaar from Chinese traders. Saltpetre is extracted from the surface soil from old stables or from under old houses. Charcoal any native can burn. The powder obtained is very course and dirty, and a large amount is required for a charge. Lead comes from China or the Shan States and is sold in the bazaars, usually four bars to the viss. It is beaten into bullets, or melted and made into shot by letting the flowing metal drop through the holes of a perforated tin placed over a bamboo filled with a thick mixture of water and cow dung. It is a primitive way to be sure, but it does the work. As all the guns are muzzle-loaders, loading and priming are done in the usual way, bits of rag or pieces of paper being used for wads.

Kachin *warfare* is now a matter of the past, as far as British Burma is concerned, but in the independent Shan States and in Chinese territory he can still enjoy what may be called the "national sport." Of warfare proper a hill-man knows nothing, but he is a skilled raider, bushwhacker and robber. Raids used to be his pastime, and a bit of fighting broke the monotony of his lonely life. The merest pretext would serve as a *casus belli,* and he went in for it with the idea of doing all the damage he could to the enemy while saving his own skin. The attacks came usually at night just before the rise of the moon. Very little real fighting was done and the blood-shed was never great. There would be a quick rush for the nearest houses, if a village was attacked; these would be set on fire, guns would be fired, and amidst a great deal of shouting prisoners and cattle would be led away, if the attack was successful. A hasty retreat would be effected, and the path would be made dangerous for the pursuers by the driving of sharp bamboo spikes in such a way that they would cut and pierce the feet of those who ventured to follow. These spikes are justly dreaded, as they inflict a most dangerous wound, and are almost invisible at night time.

Villages were never *stockaded* like the Shan or Burman; but some of the big chiefs used to have a high wall around the "palace." In time of danger all the houses situated at strategic points would be "fortified," and in stubborn fighting, if driven out of one place, they would seek shelter in the other. But the usual way of defence was to prepare some kind of a stockade on the roads leading to the village. A trench would be dug, trees put across the road, a breast-work thrown up of earth and stones, and in front of it the whole place would be studded with long and short bamboo spikes. It was seldom that any attempt was made to rush such a defence, and the usual tactics were to outflank the enemy and strike from behind. Pit-falls were often used. As they were usually very skilfully concealed great care had to be taken. They were dangerous as they were studded with sharp bamboo spikes. Traces of these pit-falls and stockades are found all over the hills, especially near the larger villages and some of them were used not so very many years ago.

A Kachin can hardly be called brave, and still he is not exactly a coward. Under leadership that he can trust he will fight bravely; but following his own method he prefers not to fight in the open. When they made an attack and found a greater resistance than expected, and things were getting "too hot," they would withdraw and wait for a better chance. Very little cruelty was practiced. Prisoners were held until redeemed, or else they were sold as slaves. They were not tortured, and the fallen were seldom mutilated. Heads might be cut off the fallen enemies to be displayed at the "dance of victory" (*pădang mănau*), but as a rule there was no such exhibition. In days gone by there was the custom of drinking some of the blood of a specially brave and ferocious enemy in order to appropriate his spirit and daring, but that belongs to the past. There are also some hints that canabalism was not unknown in those days, evidently for the same purpose. But the Kachins have long ago left these customs behind. They are not head-hunters like the Was, and their method of warfare will soon be forgotten.

The "dance of victory" has in most communities not been held for almost a generation. This wild, picturesque war-dance, reminding us of the American Indians, will probably never again be seen in its former glory in the fast changing Kachinland.

Shields of a square shape, covered with lozenge patterns, may still be seen in some communities; but they are mere curiosities and it is long since they were of any practical value.

CHAPTER IX.

SOCIAL LIFE AND AMUSEMENTS.

The social life in a Kachin community centers around such public events as a wedding or a funeral, and the customs connected with their religion. Whatever happens the whole village is concerned, and all contribute to the success of the event. When a bride makes her entrance into the community; when someone is " sent off " to the land of the dead; when there is a great sacrifice for some particular purpose; and above all, when there is a great dance (*mănau*), all come together and there is the usual feasting. But amusements in our sense of the word can hardly be said to exist, Life in the hills is mostly a keen struggle for existence; each one is hard at work to support himself. Surrounded by great natural resources, possessed of a generally fertile soil, our Kachin is poor, nearly always poorly dressed, confronted all the time with scarcity. Partial famines come very often; few have enough rice to supply them for the year. Work is to them the great reality, and as the male members of the household make it a point to do as little as possible, heavy burdens fall on the women and children.

Children at play. Child-life, as known to us, does not exist in Kachinland. The large number of deformed, half-developed and half-witted children seen in most communities of any size, is a sad commentary on social conditions. The small boys run about almost naked, amusing themselves any way they can. The broken and generally overgrown hill-sides offer no attractive play-grounds, and the youngsters grow up without any real idea of play, so important to the development of a child. Running, jumping or out-door sport in general, is almost unknown. Half-grown boys engage some in wrestling, test their strength in certain positions with bamboo poles, play marbles, a kind of "last tag," and spin tops. But there is still less of amusement for the girls. She begins work as early as possible. While yet of tender age she will carry her younger brothers or sisters, help to do the "chores," and bring water and wood. As soon as she is tall enough she begins the hard paddy-pounding, and then is sent to do her share in weeding the rice field. During the cool weather she learns to spin and weave, and she may be married before she is fifteen or sixteen, if not a mother at that age. She never has the liberty her brothers have, and the birth of a girl is regarded as something of a misfortune. When asking a Kachin how many children he has, he will always give the number of boys, the girls are not worth mentioning. Young men gamble some with cowries and dice, but not to the same extent as Shans and Burmans indulge in this pastime. They kill small birds with mud pellets shot from small bamboo bows, but this is not for sport but for something to eat.

Women. We have already mentioned the hard life imposed upon the women. They are always regarded inferior to the men. The birth of a girl is announced with, "It is only a girl." The young woman is sold for so much cash and becomes the slave of her husband and of his family, especially of the mother-in-law. It is only as she advances in years and becomes the mother of a number of sons that she becomes recognized as of any importance. If she, in addition, has some mind and strength of character she may become the virtual ruler of the household. While the women pay the heaviest price for ignorance and degrading customs, they are as a rule the more unwilling to change. It is far more difficult to induce the mother than the father to send their son to school. They cling to the old customs with a tenacity and ignorant superstition that few of the men exhibit. Centuries of servitude, hard work and no intellectual advantages, have dulled

Pounding rice. P. 88.

and blunted mind and heart, and they cannot imagine that there is anything outside their narrow world.

The young people. A visitor to a Kachin village is struck with the free and easy way of the young people. Every evening they gather at the "maidens" apartment" (*nla dap*) in some house, or else more likely in some granary decorated for the occasion with twigs and flowers. In large villages a special hut may serve the purpose, and in some instances young people from several communities may meet at some place in the jungle. The evening hours are passed with music and singing. The village bard (*lăka*) may take the lead, but it is usually done by some other young man. The singing is responsive. The young men will sing a few lines intoning or chanting the questions and the young maidens will answer. This may be kept up till midnight or later when the company breaks up and sleeping places are found wherever convenient. There are practically no restrictions in regard to the relations between young unmarried people. They are allowed to suit themselves, and the old people do not regard it as in any way improper. It is the custom, and there is nothing more to say about it. The love-songs sung at these evening gatherings have generally some immoral hints and insinuations, but not more so than many of the cheap novels freely circulated in civilized countries, or the degrading plays allowed in most communities. This custom presents the worst side of the communal life, and still we must not judge them from our standards altogether. Most Kachins admit that right here is the cause of most of their family troubles, but they are helpless against an established custom. They know of nothing else. We give the following stanzas of one of the typical love-songs, illustrating their way of looking upon the relations between the sexes. It shows us the life as lived by young people led by natural impulses and no restraining influences:

The men:

My lovely maidens, dear, beloved friends,
At this evening hour, in this amusement room
Let us exchange our lime and our tobacco;
Let our lips be coloured with the cutch and lime;
Let our mouths the love-song sing;
Let us sound forth the joyous song;
Let common laughter fill the hour.

The maidens:

Responding to the gallant song of love,
Consenting ever to the heart's desire,
If a feud be the result
And it should come to our noble brothers' ears,
The three-foot sword they'll draw,
And wield the rod and spear,
This only do we fear.

The men:

Who is the youth without a maiden?
The sprouting paddy sown and planted,
Where is the hill on which it will not grow?

The maidens:

Where is the maid without a lover?
The sprouting grain when sown and scattered,
Where is the height on which it does not grow?

The custom here described has aroused a great deal of comment from Europeans. It has been asserted more than once that no particular disgrace is attached to the young girl who becomes the mother of an illegitimate child. This is not the case. Both the girl's family and the girl herself are disgraced, and the young man in question must atone accordingly. The "mother of a bastard" has a poorer chance in marriage and brings her family a smaller sum. The child, which is generally adopted by the girl's people, is not ill-treated, but is always called a bastard. There is no attempt, however, to escape the consequences of their mistake by the use of drugs or criminal operations. That to a Kachin would be a greater wrong than the first. It should not be argued that the Kachins are especially immoral. Under ordinary restraint their young people can be as respectable as any. In the Kachin mission stations we have for nearly thirty years educated hundreds of young men and women in mixed schools. There are only one or two cases on record where pupils have actually gone wrong. In Christian villages, where the girls are kept at home and the young people in general are looked after, there are no more moral lapses than under similar conditions in civilized lands.

The village bard. Poetry is the natural speech of the savage. He thinks in similes, and his imagination is unbridled. Religious and traditional Kachin is all poetic, and in the consultation of the elders they use a great deal of high-flown poetic ideas, and quote rhymes and rhythmic proverbs which contain a great deal of imagination and insight. In most of the larger communities is a village bard (*lăka*), who is an important personage and officiates especially at weddings, when he sings the glory of the bride, and at "house-warmings," when he calls down the blessings on the occupants of the new house, wishing them happiness and prosperity. Sitting on a low stool, generally thrumming a fan to keep time, he chants the songs as inspired by the "muse" and the listeners join in the "chorus." His song has very often a real poetic strain; his flights of imagination indicate a sense of the ideal often far above what we would expect from an illiterate man living a life amidst primitive surroundings. We give here an extract from one of these songs. It is the introductory part to a wedding hymn:

O goi, agoi lo ē; on this auspicious evening,
Of me the bard, of me the youthful minstrel,
Demand the joyous task to scale the ten-span tree.
Before the youth's love-lit face place the wicker-tray:
With joyous strength I will persist, the tree I'll scale.

The grove for love songs is high above,
But I will enter the deep cool pool,
From its murky depth the fine, white sand I'll bring.
    The love-lit youth the great Creator made,
His exalted name the honoured Sun-*nat* gave,
His umbilic cord the god of wisdom shaped ;
He held the bamboo prod and opened wide his ears,
In the spacious cranium conspicious skill found room.
    And thus to every place and crowd he goes,
And sings the love-songs of the present age;
He knows no shame, its hot flame does not burn;
He need not blush nor turn his face away.
A bard is here, behold his face, amazing every one
With knowledge manifold as beads upon a bag—
A pleasant sounding violin am I.
    When in high, wild song the youth persists,
It's like as when the troubled waters from the upper springs
Soil the crystal stream from which the great chiefs drink ;
They blame the *nats* and at once bring forth
The divining bamboo to the palace front.
    Now from my sitting place I'll rise,
My bended knees I'll move,
My body's grace display;
With the crescent fan as with wings I'll play,
The ancestral story I will recount.
Once more the ancient glory I will sing.
Ye honoured elders, ye gold-producing sons,
Prepare your minds, my words receive with open ear.

Music. A double-barrelled flute made of small bamboo seems to be the only genuine musical instruments of the Kachins. Other kinds are found, but they are all of Shan or Chinese pattern. The Chinese gong is considered a necessity in a well furnished house, and the wealth of a rich man was formerly gauged by the number of gongs he possessed. The Chinese timbrel and a one-stringed violin, also of Chinese pattern, are also found; but the violin is played by very few. At the house building season, when the rice-field of a chief is to be cleared, a road or a bridge repaired, or when other communal work is on the programme, it is customary to call the people together with "music." The long Shan drum found in almost every village, one or two gongs and a pair of timbrels are in evidence, and the whole village may be marching after the musician. At other occasions it is seldom that a performance on "mixed instruments" is given. The gongs may be sounded just for the fun of it at any time, but they are mostly used when dancing the death-dance. Three gongs of different tonal power are used on this occasion. The flute and the violin enliven the evening hours when the young people meet for amusement. The Shan drum is hardly ever used except when calling the people together for communal work. At the great religious dance (*mănau*), a large cylindric drum, suspended between two heavy posts, is in use. It has a drum-head at either end, and it sends forth a strong, deep note that re-echoes among the hills, letting people far and near know the glories of the individual giving the dance. It is never used on any other occasion.

Dances and dancing. Kachins never dance for the sake of mere amusement. Anything like a "dance" or a ball is unknown. Still there are several kinds of dances, and during the cool season there is a considerable amount of dancing done by both men and women. Of course all dancing is done in oriental fashion, and the western hugging set to music is regarded as most indecent and shameful. All the dancing is connected with some religious custom, or some event from which the religious element must not be absent. (See Chap. on Mythology). Of these dances the *mănau* is the most conspicuous and characteristic. It is given only by hereditary chiefs and rich men who by special request and privilege are authorized to sacrifice to the *nat* of prosperity (*mădai nat*). Rebel chiefs (those not of the hereditary families), and ordinary commoners can never give a *mănau*. There are three kinds of this dance: the "burial dance," (*ju mănau*), the "prosperity dance" (*sut mănau*), and the "dance of victory" (*pădang mănau*). The "burial dance," which seems to be the original, is given by chiefs some time after a funeral. The original idea was to propitiate the departed. It is nowadays given by only very wealthy chiefs, and any form of the dance is now called *ju mănau,* the *ju* being simply used as a couplet of *mănau.* The "prosperity dance" is given as a thanksgiving for good fortune, for the sake of displaying one's wealth, at the same time asking the divinities for further favors. This is the most common dance. It lasts four or eight days, and costs the proprietor a great deal. The man leading the dancing is fantastically dressed, a kind of befeathered mitre (*gup du ru*), being the chief attraction of his uniform. The performance is always held on a circular dancing floor in front of the house. People come from far and near, and a great number of cattle, pigs and fowls are sacrificed and liquor flows freely. Instead of bringing the chief prosperity, it usually leaves him heavily in debt. The "dance of victory" celebrates some signal success in warfare. As Kachins can no longer fight, this dance will soon be forgotten. It is the most wild, wierd and picturesque of all their dances, and is the one given whenever they are on exhibition. Thus whatever form of dancing may be on the programme, the religious side is always present and the priest and especially the *jaiwa,* (a kind of high-priest), is the real leader. But there is enough of the "worldly" in it to satisfy any Kachin. It is a time of license, of feasting and heavy drinking, and unbridled indulgence. In the good old days there were often drunken brawls and fighting causing endless trouble and sometimes bloody feuds. When all is over and the dance is ready to break up, a cow is sacrificed, and a large yam, nicknamed a "pig," is placed near the dead animal. A supposedly crazy man, called *tsawn rawn wa,* comes and carries away the "pig" and this closes the great event. The meaning of this singular close is not clear; but it seems intended to illustrate the idea that man even though inferior to the *nats* has been able by this means, the dance, to carry away the blessings of the supernatural powers. The morning after the close of the dance a special offering, usually a white fowl, is made to the genius of "dark deeds" (*sinlai măraw*). A tall, slender tree with branches lopped off except at the top, is placed at the center of the dancing floor. It is bent as a bow by means of a stout rope and to the top branches the offering is tied. Then the rope is cut, the tree springs back and the white fowl hangs as a token that fate itself has been propitiated by the generosity and great deeds of the defrayer of the dance.

The death-dance (*kăbung dum*), is observed in the house of a departed from the time of death until it is sent off to the ancestral realms. The idea is to give the spirit (*tsu*) amusement, and incidentally to provide entertainment and consolation for those left behind. Young and old, men and women, may join in. Three gongs of different tonal power are beaten to keep time. (See Chap. XVI, para. Death-dance). The dance begins late and lasts till after midnight. It may be kept up for a long time if the family is too poor to pay the heavy expenses connected with sending the spirit to the land of the departed.

Nau Shawng or leader of dance.

House in the Hukong Valley.

CHAPTER X.

INTELLECTUAL DEVELOPMENT.

It is difficult to estimate the intellectual side of a Kachin. Of "book-learning" he has none, and still some of the older men are quite well informed. They have never had a written language, even though there is a tradition of a "lost book." This story handed down in various versions seems to be common property among illiterate tribes all over Asia, and so with the legend of the "flood." Schools and the rudiments of knowledge never enter the thoughts of our hillmen, and very few of them have patronized the Shan or Burman monasteries. Only twenty years ago I published the first book in a Romanized alphabet that had ever been seen in Kachin, and since then several hundred boys and girls have been educated in mission and Government schools. But education is still the rare exception, and the old indifference to everything along that line is the rule. The children who can be induced to enter school are bright and active and learn very quickly. The parents, especially the mothers, are nearly always opposed to the children leaving home and going to school. Many of the boys now in the schools are there without the consent of the parents. Boys of ten or eleven years of age can do as they please. They can run away and stay away. But the girls are kept more closely, and ordinarily only one girl to three boys receives an education. Some who may admit some benefits of an education for a boy, can never see the least use in a girl learning to read. She must do the work in the house, and she can pound paddy, feed the pigs and carry water without knowing the mysteries of the white man's book. Indeed a little schooling unfits her for these essentials of the domestic life. The Kachin in fact advances the same arguments in favor of ignorance that we are familiar with from other parts of the world. Yet necessity has forced him to do some thinking. Without writing, he has invented a rude form of sign language, or a system of intercommunication by giving a figurative meaning to every day objects. He has developed his calendar, and his system of measurements, reminding us of similar attempts among primitive men. He does some drawing, and has some knowledge of plants and medicine. Being used to rely mainly on the memory for everything, many have developed this faculty to a wonderful degree. The wisdom and experience of the ages has been embodied in stories and proverbs worthy of a comparision with the traditional lore of more favored and advanced races.

Sign language. Communication by the means of signs and tokens, a kind of "cipher code," is founded on the principle of "word-play." For example, *sămyit,* a needle, has for its last syllable *myit,* the word for mind or thinking. Thus a needle, sent to a distant friend means, I am thinking of you, I have you in mind. *Hpundu,* growing thatch, has for its last syllable *du,* to come, to arrive. A needle and some thatch sent together means, I am thinking of you, I will come, (or you come). *Măjap,* red-pepper, stands for *jap,* to be hot or pungent, and thus indicates anger or wounded feelings. *Dumsi prung,* a porcupine spine, contains the syllable *si* to die, hence it means death. *Shăkau,* onions, means, I will have you, from *kau,* to throw away. *Ura,* elephant bamboo, means, I desire, or love you, from *ra,* to want. Thus if a needle, some red-pepper and a piece of an onion is sent, it means, I have it in mind, I am offended, I will leave you. It will be seen that this way of communication can be both expressive and forceful.

But there are other ways to express one's feelings. Anything black (charcoal, black yarn or the like), indicates hatred, shame or destruction by fire; red indicates bloodshed and war. A miniature sword, gun or spear, made of wood, announces a declaration of war. If a notch is made in the spear and sword given at a wedding, it is especially sacred and binding. If the promise or vow is broken the offender must die by sword or spear. A piece of red yarn sent to someone means, there will be a fight; a string with one knot means, I pity you, you are alone; a knot at each end means, we are united; several knots tell the story, I will come after as many days as there are knots on the string. Anything foul-smelling indicates disgust or something vile.

Wrapping up a bundle or packet in a plantain leaf can also be made expressive of hatred or friendship. If in sending away a visitor the hostess wraps the packet in such a way that the knot is made towards her it means, I wish you could stay with us longer; if away from her, it indicates displeasure and satisfaction that he is going. When the packet is tied with bamboo splits, the number of turns indicate the mind of the giver. An even number signifies friendship and pleasure, an odd number the opposite. The greater number of turns the more the emphasis on either side.

A notched piece of bamboo is given as a pledge or a "memorandum." It is also used for keeping tally. When given as a pledge between two contracting parties it is split in two, each side keeping a half, to be compared in case of further disagreement. In time of war it was customary to send a small piece of buffalo skin, with the hair attached to it, to friends or allies asking for their assistance. When cattle were stolen some hair fastened to a piece of bamboo is stuck up somewhere along the road to indicate contempt and defiance. A small piece of spleen from a sacrificed animal would in some localities be sent to declare a feud. But many of these customs are already being forgotten, as feuds and bloodshed and intertribal wars are no longer possible because of the British rule.

Drawing. A rude kind of drawing is seen on the "prayer posts" (*lăban*), at the village entrance. It is mostly pictures of rice, ornaments and weapons, placed in this conspicuous position to remind the village divinities of what is most valuable to the inhabitants. Sometimes the front girder of a house, and the posts and girders of a *nat*-house are similarly decorated. On the graves of chiefs and rich men some decoration in Shan style is attempted, but it is all of the rudest kind imaginable. The verdict must be that the Kachins have no conception of art. Most of them cannot tell what a picture or photograph represents.

The calendar. The division of time follows the seasons of the year. The seasons are first of all divided into the dry and the wet seasons. The dry season (*ginhtawng ta*), lasts from October to March; that is, from the time of harvest to the next sowing and planting; the rainy season (*lănam ta*), is reckoned from April to September, the time when cultivation is in progress. These two divisions of the year are subdivided as follows, the New Year beginning in October:

The dry season:

Măngai ta, the time for the new rice, October and November.

Kăshung ta, the cold season, December and January.

Htawng ga ta, the hot and dry season, February and March.

The rainy season:

Nlum ta, the hot season; April to middle of May.

Htingra ta, the paddy planting season; from middle of May to the end of June.

Măyu ta, the time when paddy is growing; July to September.

The months, which are strictly lunar months, are counted from one new moon to the next. Any division into weeks is not found. The months are nearly all named after trees or flowers blossoming at certain seasons. The real Kachin names are in many localities hardly known as the Shan names are in ordinary use. The Kachin names are the following:

Kăla, October, the time when the *kăla* flower is out.

Măji, November, when the white *măji* flower is blossoming.

Măga, December, when the thorny *măga* sheds its leaves.

Hkru, January, when there is enough for all to eat.

Ra, February, when the *ra* tree is budding.

Wut, March, when the *wut* creeper is blossoming.

Shăla, April, when the *shăla* tree is in blossom.

Jăhtum, May, the end of the hot season.

Shăngan, June, the month of fevers and disease.

Shi mări, July, the wet month.

Gup shi, August, when the wet month is doubled.

Gup tung, September, when the wet months are at their height.

If the Kachin names are not used, as is the case in many localities, the Shan names take their place. These are, beginning with October, *Lunjing, Lungam, Lunsam,* etc., the word *lun,* month, with the numerals up to twelve. In the Northern Shan States these names are everywhere used.

The hours of the day indicate the progress of the sun and well known natural phenomena. Counting from midnight we have—

Yup tung, 12 o'clock, time of deep sleep.

Hpung tsin se, 1–2 a. m., time of the quiet morning breeze.

U goi, 3 a. m., the cock crow.

Ginhtawng pru, 4 a. m., the rise of the morning star.

Mănap, 5 a. m., the time of dawn.

Jan pru, 6 a. m., sunrise.

Jan dahkaw mi lung, 7 a. m., the sun ascended the length of a weaving board.

Jan tsing law tsan, 8–11 a. m., forenoon, when the sun is quite high.

Jan pungding ga, 12 m., the sun cleaveng the top of the head.

Jan kăyau, 1–2 p. m., the sun on the descent, "recline."

Jan kădang, 3–4 p. m., the sun "tumbling down," rapidly descending.

Jan nmaw mi rawng, 5 p. m., the sun at the height of a may-pole.

Jan shang mădu, 6 p. m., the sun about to go down, to enter.

Nrim, 7 p. m., the evening dusk.

Shang tawn, 8–9 p. m., the time when all are inside their houses.

Pran tawm, 10–11 p. m., the time when the young people amuse themselves.

It should be remembered that the Kachin's idea of time is exceedingly vague and indefinite. His year is, roughly speaking, from one paddy harvest to another, his month from new moon to new moon, and his day from sunrise to sunrise. They can never tell their ages with certainty, and in regard to old persons they make the wildest guesses. Any old man between seventy and eighty is always thought of as a hundred years old. The fact that it is an honor to be very old has something to do with this; but as there are no ways of reckoning except keeping in mind the harvest season, it is easy to see how they soon become confused. Anything like an intercalary month or period is unknown, and they have no fixed number of days in their year. Whether there are twelve or thirteen new moons between one harvest and the next is never thought of, they simply follow the coming and going of the seasons.

Of the stars the Kachins have a superstitious dread and they never dare to count them or point at them, without some way of circumlocution. The morning star (*mănap ginhtawng*), and the pleiades (*kru măjan*), are the only stars named. This last constellation, when at a certain height, is regarded as indicating the time when paddy should be sown.

Measures. Measures of length are as follows:

Lămyin chyang, the length of the black of the nail.

Lăywng tsen, one finger's width.

Lăhkawng pren, two fingers' width.

Măsum pren, three fingers' width.

Măli pren, four fingers' width.

Lăhpa mi, the width of the hand.

Gumdun, from the end of the thumb to the end of the first finger.

Gumchyan, or *lăhkam,* a span, reckoned from the thumb to the end of the second finger.

Lătup dawng, from the elbow to the knuckles of the fist.

Dawng mi, from the elbow to the second finger's tip.

Sinda ga, from the finger's tip to the middle of the chest.

Lălam, a fathom.

Measures of capacity are nowadays determined by the standards in the Shan, Chinese or Burman localities nearest to them. The small and the large basket may be used in the same place; each community is at liberty to have its own standards and the headman alone can interfere if the measures are not of the prescribed capacity. The generally accepted measures are as follows:

Lătup mi, one handful,—the hand nearly closed.

Lăpai mi, one open handful, two *lătup.*

Lăku mi, as much as can be held in both hands.

Jăre mi, four handfuls.

Bye mi, four *jăre.*

Jik mi, four *byi,* a fourth of a basket.

Hpai mi, the half of a basket; two *jik.*

Dang mi, one basket, about one bushell.

Jaw mi, ten baskets.

Weights. The standards in weights are even more variable than those of measures. The Chinese and Shan scales are used, and the Chinese balance, or steel-yard, is not uncommon. The following are the ordinary weights:

Lem mi, the weight of one *mălem,* a kind of seed.

Dum mi, a stone or piece of metal equal to two *mălem.*

Pe mi, equal to two *dum.*

Mu mi, the eighth of a viss.

Gahkan, the half of a viss.

Joi mi, one viss, (3.6 pounds).

Money. In counting money the Kachins follow the Shans. Copper coin was formerly not accepted in the hills but now it is taken everywhere. The use of Chinese bullion is now a thing of the past, but a good deal of uncoined silver is still found. Many of the more wealthy have bags of it concealed in safe places. The names of pieces of currency vary somewhat is different localities, but the following will be accepted and understood everywhere:

Ka mi, one pie.

Hpaisan or *peksan,* one pice.

Pe mi, one anna.

Mu mi, two annas; a two-anna bit.

Hti mi, four annas, a four-anna bit.

Lap mi or *gyap mi,* one rupee; in the Shan States often called *bya mi.*

Rawng mi, two and a half rupees.

Hkan mi, ten rupees.

Gahkan, fifty rupees; half a viss of silver.

Pan mi, seventy-five rupees; three-fourths of a viss of silver.

Joi mi, one hundred rupees; one viss of silver.

Numbers. There are different names for the cardinals, 1 to 10, 20, 100, 200, 1000, and 10,000; but a Kachin has no clear idea of numbers above a thousand. When he wishes to convey the idea of anything innumerable and thus incomprehensible, he uses the expression, thousand and tens of thousands (*hkying mi mun mi*). For larger figures he borrows Shan or Burman terms, but they convey no meaning to him whatsoever. Even children who have been in school a number of years find it difficult to understand what is meant by a hundred thousand and a million. Either only stands for something that cannot be counted.

Plants and medicine. Our hillman has names for most of the things growing in the jungle. He uses a number of plants, roots and herbs for medicinal purposes; but most of his drugs he gets from the Shans and the Chinese. It

Drawing water.

P. 104.

is only in the case of sores, ulcers and the like, that he applies remedies. In more severe cases he is a "faith-healer," believing that his sacrifices and prayers to the spirits will bring the desired help. In European medicine he has a very uncertain faith. He will try it when everything else has failed. And even if he takes it he is likely to use the native mixtures on the sly. He can't see how there can be any virtue in a sugar-coated pill that tastes sweet and pleasant as it goes down. He wants something that will choke him; something the taste of which will remain for at least a week. The viler the stuff the more effective it is sure to be; the worse it tastes the more satisfied he is. Among other drugs, the blood of wild buffalo, the gall of a python, the fat and gall of the slow-loris, crushed tiger's bones, musk, and the gall of the bear are especially valued in Kachin pharmacy.

Proverbs. Like other orientals the Kachins have embodied the wisdom of the ages in a number of proverbs and pithy sayings. Some of them are very apt and to the point and carry a meaning even in translated form. We give a few, the originals of which are found in the Kachin Spelling Book and in the Introduction to the Dictionary.

The priest grabs for a comb,—of which he has no need, his head being shaved; said of inordinate and unreasonable greed.

The Chinaman's offering the fowl's head,—this being a rare delicacy and only one in the dish, no one out of courtesy will accept it, and so he can eat it himself.

I believe, but only as I believe a visitor,—whom it is polite not to contradict.

Having fallen from the granary you raise the ladder.

Measure the pig before you make the basket.

The pigeon left and the crow took its place.

When the lamp is lit you must expect insects.

The humming bird's eggs are naturally small.

Hit the horn, the ear quivers.

If bamboo or wood is crooked it can be seen, a crooked mind no one can see.

When saying, "Work, work," I alone hear it; when calling, "Come and eat," a flock of monkeys gather.

There is a bazaar for selling salt and fish, but none for selling brothers and sisters.

It is for a slave to obey, for a goat to eat ferns.

Rocky places are the natural home for goats.

No one can change his colour, anyone can repent.

When children trade, men lose.

Anyone can set fire to a prairie or kill a Shan.

He who sees a trout will let the crab go.

Everyone sees the hole in the other man's bag, no one sees it in his own.

The paddy planting season we know, but man's time we cannot tell.

The language is rich in this kind of sayings and is easily adapted to similies and figurative forms of speech.

Riddles. (*Gumwai ga.*) Riddles and veiled sayings are also numerous; but it is necessary to know Kachin customs and ways in order to understand them. We will give only two or three examples of the most characteristic:

What is the elephant always in a paddy-field? The paddy house.

What is always crying when men pass? The door.

What has porcupine holes by the shore line? The nose.

What is always carrying around a basket of "bamboo-spikes"? The porcupine.

What is it that says, "Mother, I will go first"? The hand-spindle,—referring to the custom of the women always to use the hand-spindle (*hkăbang*) as they walk along.

A great deal of the difficulty in understanding native conversation is due to ignorance of customs and usages constantly alluded to. A Kachin takes it for granted that you must know all he knows about their ways and habits, family relations and everything else. His world is in very many respects entirely the opposite of ours; but he must be excused for not being able to understand this. Few Europeans ever learn to understand the native mind; there is always a gulf fixed between the east and the west. It is not surprising that the white man, with his strange ways and customs so different from anything the oriental mind has ever conceived, is forever a riddle and a mystery, especially to our uncivilized hillmen with their narrow vision and perspective. It takes long years and study for a European to get so familiar with the natives that he can think as they think and understand their point of view. But however close he gets, there will always be something that will escape him, some things that he will never fully understand.

CHAPTER XI.

MYTHOLOGY AND TRADITIONS.

Like all primitive people our Kachins are fond of stories and story-telling. If all their traditional lore was collected, it would make a volume strange and interesting. They do not have the imagination of the Arabian Nights, nor the insight into the mysteries of nature shown in Indian myths; but they carry with them traces of the earliest attempts of primitive man to account for the world around him. Nearly every incident, experience and phenomenon of life can be illustrated and explained by some story, tradition or myth, indicating their faith, ideas and conception of nature. In many of them we trace a close relationship to similar stories among other tribes and races. Some have travelled a long road before they assumed the shape the Kachin story-teller gives them. In all we can see how the human mind naturally travels along certain channels, and how the phenomena of nature everywhere receive nearly the same explanation when man has nothing to guide him but his limited observation and untrained imagination. We cannot in a single chapter do justice to all their traditions and curious tales, but we will select a few that will help us to understand Kachin belief in regard to the past and present, the seen and the unseen. Most of these stories I have had printed in the Kachin Spelling Book, the first Reader, and Introduction to the Grammar and Dictionary.

The Creation. The savage is as interested as the man of science in the beginning of things. When the great religious dance (*mănau*) is given, the professional story-teller (*jaiwa*), rehearses the whole creation-legend as handed down by the Kachins. It is told in rhythmic, sometimes truly poetic, language. We can give it here only in a condensed form. Originally, "before the beginning," there was no heaven or earth. There existed only wind, clouds, and a mysterious female half human and half avian. From these agencies were brought forth by a generative process the first cosmic matter and the primitive spirits. The first spirits, *Kringkrawn* and *Kringnawn,* brought forth the first seven *nats* (lower forms of spirits), the names of which are borne by the first seven sons in every family where that number or more are born. This mysterious pair also gave birth to the first reptiles, birds and wild animals. Having thus in eight successive births given existence to the primitive *nats* and first animal life, the earth itself was given form and order, but the present division of land and water came much later. Two great spirits, *Chyănun* and *Woishun,* now appeared—exactly from where is not clear. *Chyănun* gave birth to nine new *nats,* and at nine successive births brought forth the elemental parts of our world. After each birth she again became a "maiden" (or a virgin), and having nine times returned to maidenhood, she bore *Hpung Un* and *Hpung An,* after which she became the mother of the "nine brothers," who play a very important part in Kachin traditions. At last she gave birth to a monstrous being named *Ninggawn wa Măgam.* The mother was in birth-pain for seven years, and he held at his birth a great hammer and a pair of tongs. (In *Chyănun* we have a personification of the life-producing process of nature.) *Ninggawn wa,* with the tools in his possession, gave the present form and shape to Kachin-land. He began at *Măjoi Shingra Bum* (the Eden of Kachin tradition), and has to his credit only the territory east of the Irrawaddy as far south as the *Loi sip sam,* the "thirty mountains," just south of Kutkai. Having finished this, nevertheless, tremendous task he planned to build a bridge across the Irrawaddy a few miles north of Myitkyina. But the "nine brothers," out of malice or envy because of the great achievements of their really younger brother, caused the work to cease, and *Ninggawn wa* sent the Flood.

Having given birth to *Ninggawn wa* his mother (*Chyănun*) brought forth a great pumpkin which the "Omniscient One," (apparently the last of *Chyănun's* sons), divided into two parts after the death of the mother. From the part to the right the first man was created, from the left half came the first woman. This happy pair dwelt at the central part of the earth, by a beautiful mountain created from the head of *Chyănun*. This in brief is the Kachin creation story. Variations and local colourings are found reflecting Shan or Chinese influence, but this must be expected where the only authority is an oral tradition and everyone is allowed full liberty in imagination and fancy. The whole creation story given in its minute details would fill a small volume. We give here a free translation of the introductory part as rehearsed by a high-priest (*jaiwa*) at exceptionally great occasions.

Formerly the heavens high were not,
The stable earth had no existence.
Where since were fixed the heavens high,
The fleeting cloud alone appeared.
Where now the solid earth is seen,
The fairy-fowl alone was found.
The fleeting cloud in haste descended
Covering the fowls short tail.
In haste she bore, at once gave birth,
Something like a wicker-basket was born,
Something like a capsule of a plant.
She filled the basket, packed the capsule,
It became the size of a waiter,
In circumference as a fanning-tray.
Thus the cloud *nat* Earth appeared;
The Earth of the Fairy-fowl became.
Then was born *Kringkrawn*,
And after him *Kringnawn*.
Then the fleeting cloud expired,
All existing lands it heard,

But close to heaven hung the drooping clouds.
The Fairy-fowl also expired.
Informed are existing lands,
But then appeared the bird *Lătsaw*.

The bird *Lătsaw* seems to be a Kachin phoenix, but no one seems to know definitely its history. Just as the rain-giving clouds take the place of the first original cloud, so this mysterious bird appears when the first fowl expires. Again we see the trend towards personification.

The Great Flood, (Shăn Shăing). The Kachin version of this almost universal story is the following. Sometime after *Minggawn wa* had finished his creative work and appointed dwelling places for the different races, he started to build a huge stone bridge across the Irrawaddy, the foundation of which can still be seen a few miles north of Myitkyina. His nine brothers, already mentioned, moved with envy because of the great achievements of their younger brother, determined to undo the work. So they came one day and said to him, "Your mother is dead, return home." This did not seriously trouble him, as he thought it would be easy to find a step-mother. Having failed the first time the brothers made a second attempt, saying, "Your father is dead, come back." This caused him great sorrow and "his royal heart was filled with anger," as he realized that no one could take the place of a father. He crushed in his wrath an adjacent mountain and returned home. Arriving at the palace he found both father and mother well and hearty. Realizing that he had been deceived, he determined to take vengeance on his brothers. He caused a great deluge intending to extinguish every form of life. The brothers, however, were not drowned, but were afterwards killed by a viper. But all other human beings were killed except two orphans who escaped in a large, oval shaped drum. They took along nine cocks and nine steel needles. A needle was dropped and a cock let lose each passing day. On the ninth day,

Manau altars.

P. 112.

they heard the needle ring against the stones, and the last cock crow. Then they knew that the earth was dry. One of the orphans was some time after their escape killed by a ferocious demon. The other one married a half-demon named *Nănghkut* (smoke). They had a child which was killed by a cruel spirit, named *Jăhtung,* when the mother was absent from home. The spirit prepared the liver for the mother to eat, and the body was chopped into small pieces and scattered over an adjoining field. From this strange seed a new race grew up, somewhat different from the antediluvian, the one now inhabiting the world.

The story of the origin of the new race runs as follows in a somewhat different version in which the *Jăhtung* and the field are absent. The two orphans married and had a child. When old enough to be weaned the child was left in the care of an old man while the parents were out at work. The child cried for the mother and the old man said, "What if I cut up (lit., mine) the child and scatter (lit., sow) the pieces at the nine cross-roads"? The child understanding the meaning of his words kept quiet. But one day the old man carried out his fearful threat. Having disposed of the pieces at the cross-roads, he took the liver and some of the intestines and prepared a broth; to deceive the mother he covered a low stool with the garments of the child. When the mother returned after dark she asked for her child. The old man said, "Your child is asleep; sit down and eat this broth and I will bring it." The mother did as she was told. Having finished her meal the old man told her, "You have eaten your child," and informed her what he had done. The mother in despair went to the "nine cross-roads." Then she saw that from her child had grown up nine different races. She came to the first and exclaimed, "Oh, my child!" This one said, "You have eaten our intestines and liver, we are afraid of you." She came to the second, repeating the same words, and received the same answer. Each one in turn showed that they were afraid of her, and did not regard her as the true mother. Then in sadness and sorrow she departed to the country where the sun goes down. But before she left she instructed them how to sacrifice to her in case they became afflicted with disease. This is the reason why now "all men" make offerings to the *Janhku,* the spirit causing bowel-trouble.

Origin of death. Man was born immortal, but because of a foolish desire to play with death, and deceive the spirit holding the "cord of life," illness, old age and decease were imposed as a punishment by the "Spirit of the Sun." The story, which is one of the most instructive and characteristic in Kachin traditional lore, is told in various ways. I give it here mainly as printed in the Kachin Reader, differing somewhat from the version followed in the Spelling Book. Formerly when there were nine suns and dogs grew nine tails, death was unknown among men. Grass and weeds only died, and there was simply an appearance of burial, when they decayed and again became dust. Then the great trees began to grow old and die, last of all the mighty banyan, but there were no funeral ceremonies; the trunk remained above ground and was allowed to decompose and decay. Just about this time the first old and venerated elephant drew his last breath in the midst of the jungle; all the animals of the forest came in mourning and said, "Oh, our grandfather!" Only the goat came and said, "Ah, my grandson!" Now the sun went up and down, and every time the great luminary sank in the west men said, "The sun is dead," and went to the land of the sun to dance the death-dance. The other version has it, that as there were nine suns the heat was unbearable, and by complaining to the sun-*nat* one sun after the other was extinguished until only one remained. The men at the expiration of each sun went and danced the death-dance. Having on eight different occasions danced in the sun-country, mankind, wishing to return the attention paid to them, invited the sun-*nats* for a similar performance in a human abode. The spirit of the sun who holds the "cord of life," testing the cord found it was not broken, and hence knew that no one had died. Still they all went, and danced the death-dance all night long. In the morning, when outside the house, about to return they said to each other, "We have danced the death-dance all night long, but we have seen no corpse." So re-entering the house they put bird-lime (or wax) on their feet and as they danced, everything stuck to their feet and at last was exposed a large squirrel, "with glazed eyes and shining teeth," dressed up as a corpse. The sun-spirits now returned to the great mother-spirit reporting what they had seen. Then said the sun-spirit, "No one has died among men, but as they wish to die let the cord of life be cut for old men and women." The other version is here more graphic; when the sun-spirits saw the deception practiced on them they said, "Well, if men wish to die let old men and women expire." Returning home they passed the abode of the headman of *Măjoi Shingra,* the chameleon, who holds about the same place in Kachin tradition as the serpent among the Semitic races. Hearing their foot-steps he asked where they had been and what they had done. Being informed he asked, "And what did you decide"? They answered, "Old people must die." "No" said the chameleon, "since you left, my son *Ahtoi rawng* (the light-bearer) has died, and my decree is that old and young must die without distinction." But even now men did not die as at present. A very old woman, *Mări nang,* was the first to die and they made her a coffin. She told her people, " When I die you will see me disappear by the corner of the fire-place." As she had told them so it happened; the moment she died her people saw her disappear by the corner, and being frightened they ran to the opposite side. Seeing this she said, "Are then my children and grandchildren really afraid of me?" She then drew a spirit-veil over their eyes, and since then no human being has ever seen a disembodied spirit.

There were no funeral ceremonies made when *Mări nang* died.

Then *Kăbang Gumna* died and they introduced the proceedings that are now customary on such occasions. But they did not know what music to furnish when dancing the death-dance. Hearing the owl they caught the idea of the deep, solemn tones of the "three gongs." They did not know how to dance the "spear-dance" in front of the house, but seeing the hole of the mole, and how he arranged his pieces of roots, they learned to finish with care the spear representing the wealth and prosperity of the house; while the spear representing the world of the dead is left unfinished with the ends of the bamboo splits, with which it is wound, sticking out in every direction. Thus the children of *Kăbang Gumna* perfected the funeral ceremonies. Having buried her, these ceremonies were observed by *Wahkyet wa,* and his wife *Măgawng kăbang măjan.* When they grew old and were ready to depart hence, they ordered their children to bury them with the now ancestral ceremonies and customs. Another version says that the death-dance and the now accepted customs were observed for the first time when a certain *Lădu wa Pungngang* ended his life.

The loss of the Fruit of Life. When men had become mortal a number of cattle came and devoured the "life-giving fruit" which otherwise would have kept the human race immortal. When mankind complained, the cattle promised to be willing always to be sacrificed in their behalf. Thus are cattle offered as substitutes for men in case of illness or other calamities.

The lost Book. The story of a lost book is universal among the illiterate races of Burma. Just what is behind the tradition is impossible to say, but it may in the case of the Karens, at least, represent a faint echo of a higher form of civilization in days gone by than they now possess. The Kachin rendering of this interesting episode is as follows. "When the world had been set in order and the different races assigned their respective homes, *Ninggawn wa Măgam*, after having built a house on the *Shăjang* mountain, and a dancing floor on the *Sumhpan* plain, and after having propitiated all the fates, called the children of men together and informed them that now he was ready to return to his great central palace. The tribes of men implored him to remain, as without him they would be helpless. This request he could not grant, but he gave to the wild boar his tusks, and to the hornbill its gorgeous plumage. Likewise for the help of mankind he gave to each race a book. The Chinese received a book on paper; the Shans and Burmans books of palm-leaves, to foreigners he also gave paper books, but the Kachins received a book of parchment. On the return the recipient of the Kachin book prepared and ate it, either to appease his hunger or else because he thought this the best way to preserve it. (This point is not quite clear.) But at all events since that day the Kachins have had no written book; the great priests and story-tellers keep its contents in their minds (lit. in their stomachs), and repeat it all at the great feasts, when it takes three days and nights to rehearse it. It contains the only authentic record of creation, the flood, different human races, the origin of the *nats* (spirits), and tells us all about their work and worship.

Why the Kachins are nat (spirit) worshippers. When the great *Ninggawn wa* once called all the races together, the Kachin men brought with them the ordinary large holed wicker basket, while the other races brought their closed baskets. It happened that this was the time gold, silver and other riches were to be distributed to the children of men. Shans, Burmans, Chinese and foreigners filled their baskets and carried them home; the gold and silver fell out between the holes of the Kachin baskets, and only the more worthless articles remained. This is the reason the Kachins are poor, as compared with more favored nations. One version of the story says the Kachins carried only their bags, or haversacks, and that accounts for the small amount of money a Kachin possesses. Next time the races were called together the Kachins thought they would profit by their former misfortune, and instead of carrying the ordinary man's basket were armed with the closed baskets carried by women. The other races in some way were aware of the particular nature of the gift awaiting them, and so came with large holed wicker baskets. This time *nats* (spirits) were distributed. The Kachin's baskets were filled and the *nats* could not escape, while they dropped out through the holes as soon as poured into the baskets of the other nations. The Kachin load was exceedingly heavy, and they had to stop now and then along the road to lighten the burden by letting out some of the *nats*. But they reached home with about half of the number. To these they now must offer in their homes and villages. The others must be propitiated whenever they are on the road, as these spirits are encountred everywhere, being somewhat lonely among their solitary hills or on the plains.

Natural phenomena. Everything in the realm of nature has a supernatural cause, and is attributed to the agency of some powerful demon or spirit. Rain and clouds are caused by the celestial *nat,* and the reverberation of the thunder is the warning of his voice. There is nothing before which a Kachin stands in greater awe than thunder and lightning. It is to him expressive of the greatest imaginable power in the upper regions. The rainbow comes from the mouth of an immense crab, inhabiting subterranean caves. Once in a while it comes out and then the "great swing" (*n-goi la tum,*) appears. If the arc is complete it is not likely to rain the day following; if it is "broken," or very faint, "it may or may not rain," which is a safe prognostication, quite characteristic, and typical of predictions in general. Another rendering has it that the rainbow is caused by a great woman washing a variegated skirt the colors of which are running. This is simpler than the crab story and to the average mind more satisfactory.

An eclipse is caused by a tremendous frog trying to swallow the sun, (*jan shu măyu,*) or the moon (*shăta shu măyu*). In some localities, especially near the Chinese frontier, gongs are beaten, guns are fired, and the people cry at the top of their voices, "Let it go! let it go!" to frighten away the frog trying to do away with the luminary. It is always a wonder how an eclipse can be foretold months and years ahead. When they are convinced that it can be done, their one explanation is that the spirits must in some way make it known to the white man.

An earth-quake is explained in at least three different ways. One tradition states that once upon a time the large beetle (*kindu nan,*) came and lied to the earth-spirit called *măn hpădam,* and said: "The men on the top of the earth are all dead, I am unable to bury them." So in order to find out she shook the pillars of the earth. A somewhat related rendering is the following: "Once in a while when things are too peaceful and quiet on the surface of the earth, the terrestrial spirit says, "I wonder if my children have forgotten me, or if they are all dead." So in order to satisfy herself she shakes her umbrella, and the earth feels the effect. It is thus customary to call out at an earth-quake, *Dum să ga ai law,* "We remember you," signifying that they are neither dead nor guilty of forgetfulness. In some localities the movements of subterranean alligators are regarded as the cause, and the oriental story of a mighty serpent coiled around the world, biting its own tail and in the agony shaking the foundations of the world, is also told. But these last legends can be traced back to Shan and Chinese sources. The alligator, however, plays an important part in Kachin mythology, but in this instance the first two stories are no doubt the most truely Kachin.

Some of these stories seem to be common property among all the hill tribes. The Manipur Nagas are in the habit of shouting, "We are alive," whenever an earthquake happens, for about the same reason that moves a

Kachin to call out, "We remember you." Instead of the Kachin beetle, some Naga tribes, according to T. S. Hodson, attribute to a grasshopper the dismal story that no men were left upon the earth. In fact all these nature myths can be traced back to a common origin, if we can only go back far enough. The forces of nature are naturally deified. What is so far beyond the power of man, must be the work of some god, spirit or demon. The story of the Demiurge is as old and universal as mankind; it is told in the words of the savage, as well as in the scientific language of civilized man. Primitive man believes in the wonderful and supernatural without a word of questioning. He feels the need of some explanation of what he sees and hears, feels and fears; and the assurance that behind it all dwells the power that rules over all, the divinities and spirits that everywhere encompass him, is quite sufficient for his intelligence. That these divinities are the creation of his own imagination never occurs to him. It is from simple stories of this kind that many of our most interesting legends, myths and traditions have grown. The Greek and the Roman, the Hindu and the Chinaman, see the same world, and left to themselves, explain it very much the same way.

The shaded parts of the moon come from the foliage of an immense banyan, or India-rubber tree. This tree is held in reverence on account of its size and the general belief that they are inhabited by *nats*. All the tribes of Burma, as well as most of the inhabitants of India and China, regard this useful shade tree as sacred. No doubt Buddhist influence has had a great deal to do with this.

The universe is divided into its three natural divisions: the heavens above (*Mătsaw Ntsang*), the earth (*Dinghta ga*), and the underworld (*Kătsan ga*). But with many the *Kătsan ga*, "the far off country," is identical with *ji woi ga*, the ancestral realms, or *jatna ga*, the gathering place of the dead. But this question we will discuss more fully in

A myihtoi or prophet ascending the platform. P. 120.

the chapter on funeral ceremonies and the belief in the hereafter.

Origin of the religious dance (*mănau*). We have in a previous chapter given an account of this the greatest of Kachin events. How it originated is told as follows: In the beginning no one knew the dance. Only the sun-*nats* knew the secret and when they danced they called the birds to participate. The birds accordingly went to the sun-country and learned the dance. Returning they saw a banyan tree with ripe fruit. The black-bird skipping about said, "Let us eat." The *Npring* bird also began to dance and said, "Let us eat." Thus while partaking of the fruit the birds danced the dance of the sun-country. Then imitating the birds a man *Shingra wa Gumja* (the all around good man of the central country), and his wife, *Mădai num Hpraw* (the white celestial woman), learned the dance and introduced it among men.

The first man to die of snake-bite. Once an escaped prisoner discovered the hole of a snake. That night he slept with some snake-charmers and told them what he had seen. Then they urged him, "Show us the place;" but he replied, "I am afraid." Then they said, "Show us the place and you can marry our sister." Besides urging, the youngest brother took a bamboo and cut it up in pieces about a yard long indicating that thus he would deal with the snake. The next older cut the pieces about a foot long, signifying his superior contempt for the reptile. The oldest, the bravest of all, cut the pieces a hand-breadth, typifying how he would make "mince-meat" of any snake however large. Thus exhibiting their power, the man was induced to show them the place. As they stood by the hole one of the snakes came out. The oldest brother tried to hit the snake; but the sword flew to pieces. The others fared no better. Being thus disarmed the brothers were drawn into the hole and killed. From that time on men have died from snake-bite.

How fire was discovered. Once upon a time two men

named *Numlang* and *Kumhtan* saw smoke arise the other side of a river named *Hkrang hka.* Trying to cross, *Numlang* was carried down-stream but *Kumhtan* succeeded, and eventually reached the place of the fire. There he saw two *nats* in human shape named *N Tu* and *N Htu,* man and wife. The weather was cold and feeling the heat from the flame he asked them to show him the secret of the fire. They consented, and promised that if ever the fire went out in his home or village, a couple bearing their names should by rubbing bamboo pieces together be able to produce fresh fire. *Kumhtan* departed with his secret and after some time found his lost companion in a village where fire had never been seen. He gathered some wood and kindled a fire, but being inexperienced they set the whole village on fire. From this time on such accidents have ever happened.

The first man burned to death. Some time after the incident just described, the children of the swine were preparing a fishing-dam. The rat-catchers and fish-catchers (all of them *nats*) were also there. Then said *Ninggawn wa* to the children of men, "You go and catch the fish." The rat-catchers and the others heard it, and after a certain *Mauhte wa* had crossed the bridge they severed some of the bamboos, so when *Mauhte wa* tried to return the bridge broke and floated down on the dam. There a certain widower sat drying his cloth by a fire, and the timber of the broken bridge caught fire and *Mauhte wa* perished. After that the house of a rich family caught fire and several perished; the spirit of *Mauhte wa* has ever since been abroad and is implicated in every accidental fire.

From these legends have originated the particular customs observed in the case of a fire. After a house has burned, every fire in the village is extinguished. A certain individual impersonates the traditional *Mauhte wa.* With a smoking-pipe in his mouth and a bag full of ashes from the burned house in his hand, he goes around the ruined house proclaiming that he is *Mauhte wa* the *nat* of accidental or incendiary fire. Completing the fourth round he is driven away with stones and sticks and chased to the nearest stream where he drops his bag of ashes, placing large stones on it. A vessel containing water is buried in some hill near the entrance of the village so as to keep the fire-spirit away. A priest is in the meantime propitiating the genius of fire, "that ought to be a friend, but has proved to be an enemy." When all is ready, a man named *N Tu* and a woman named *Ma Htu,* are selected in accordance with the instruction of the spirits at *Hkrang hka.* They rub pieces of bamboo together and thus produce fresh fire. From this fire all the family hearths are rekindled. (As an *N Tu* may also be called *Tu Lum,* and a *Ma Htu* may go by the name of *Htu Lum,* their names are also given in this story as *Tu Lum* and *Htu Lum*).

A somewhat different ceremony is followed in case, as is quite customary, the site of the destroyed house is sprinkled. In that case the proceedings are the following: A water ditch lined with plantain sheets is made from the higher side of the site. The water runs down to the lower side where *Mauhte* is standing. He is dressed in red, with a smoking cigar made of plantain leaves in his mouth; he holds a fire-brand in one hand and a small fowl tied to a string in the other. When the priest is through with his incantations, he turns to *Mauhte* and asks, "Who are you?" *Mauhte* replies:

"I am *Mauhte,* the hero with the broken sword,
I have taken the broken sword and killed a man,
I lighted my cigar and put fire to a house."

Then he goes around the house seven times. At the seventh time the village people, who have been lying in wait for him, rush towards him and say, "So you are *Mauhte?* You fired the house, did you?" Then they drive him off with "spears" made of reeds. He runs to some ravine, where he drops his fire-brand. He is then stripped of his red clothing, and his cigar is taken away from him. All of it is thrown into the stream and the party returns home.

A one-day holiday is always declared after a fire when no work must be done, and those who feel so inclined propitiate the "fates." But there is considerable diversity in regard to ceremonies observed on such occasions, and many localities have some items all their own. But there is always something connected with the legend of *Mauhte* and his doings. In him we have a personification of the "fire-spirit" viewed as an enemy and not a friend of man.

The first men killed by accident. Long ago a certain man named *Lăhtwi* had a son and a daughter. There lived also two men named, respectively, *Lăbyu* and *Lămyam.* The father wanted the last named for his son-in-law, but the daughter favored *Lăbyu* and he became her husband, At this juncture a winged monster named *Lăhkwi Yawng* captured and carried off the woman. The husband went everywhere looking for his wife. First of all he met a man named *Myihkyi măgun,* ("dirty-eye"), and asked him, "Have you seen the *Lăhtwi* woman?" Dirty-eye replied, "If you ever find your wife again the dirt in my eye will be enough to poison the whole of the Irrawaddy." Then he went on and met a man named *Shinglang gălu,* ("long-leg," lit. long-shin), and asked him the same question. Long-leg contemptuously replied, "If you ever find your wife, let me know and my shins will bridge the river." Then he saw a man named *Pungwum wa,* ("frowzy-head"), and asked him for information. Frowzy-head laughingly said, "If you ever find your wife my head will burn for nine whole years." At last he came to the Hornet enquiring for his lost wife. The Hornet by a fine thread led him to a cave where the woman was held a prisoner. As *Lăbyu* entered he discovered his wife, and found that the monster was out hunting. Then the woman told him, "Make your sword red-hot, and be ready when *Lăhkwi Yawng* returns from the hunt; as soon as he comes in he will spread out his wings and go to sleep." *Lăbyu* did as he was told. Presently the monster appeared, and as he entered he scented the visitor and said, "I smell the flesh of a *Jinghpaw.*" The woman replied, "Are you not living with a *Jinghpaw* woman?" Then he spread out his wings and fell asleep. *Lăbyu* with his red-hot sword quickly severed the right wing from his body and fled with his wife. The monster in vain tried to fly with only one wing. From that time on men have had the misfortune to be disabled by the loss of arms or legs. *Lăbyu,* returning with his wife, first met Frowzy-head, and as he did not have hair enough to supply fuel for even a day, he was killed. Thus men will die from burning. Then he saw Long-leg, who in vain tried to bridge the Irrawaddy with his shins, and he was killed. So men will die from recklessness. Dirty-eye met the same fate on account of his rash bravado. From this time on men have met a similar fate. Now the *Lăhtwi* girl wanted to eat some fruit. *Lăbyu* climbed a tree to cut down some, but the spirits of the murdered men directed his sword to cut off his arms, legs and neck. When the woman saw what had happened she said, "Now what will I do?" Her dead husband answered, "Place a knife between some small branches, then whistle for the wind and follow me." (The idea being that the wind, responding to the whistling, would come and shake the branches, causing the knife to fall and kill her). This she did and from that time on men have died from murder, by the instigation of the spirits and in the desire to follow the departed.

The first man drowned. Once upon a time an orphan walking along a stream saw a big worm boring into a tree. He cut out the borer and gave relief to the tree. Fishing in the stream he cast his net over an alligator. Being unable to pull him out he tied the rope of the net to a tree and returned home. The next day the alligator's daughter, realizing the sad plight of her father, went to the tree and asked, "Who helped you out of your trouble?" The tree replied, "The orphan boy." Hearing this she asked the tree to inform her when the orphan boy would be around. The day after that he came and the daughter was called. Seeing the boy she said to him, "You helped the tree, can you not help my father also?" The boy with an eye to his own advantage said," If I do it what will you give me?" The daughter promised to marry him provided he relieved her father. Then the boy by degrees pulled the alligator out of the river and on the seventh day relieved him from the net. True to her promise the daughter married the boy and they made their home by the river. Having lived together for some time the wife one day said to her husband, "All the fish in the river are my brothers, do not fish with the nine brothers." He however disobeyed, and went with them a fishing, deciding neither to eat nor take home any fish. When the nine brothers saw that he refused to accept any fish, they, out of mischief, secretly put a small stone-sucker in his bag. Returning home his wife accused him saying, "You have been a fishing with the nine brothers, I smell my relatives." He denied the charge, and as a proof that he had no fish turned his bag inside out, and the small fish fell out. Then the wife in grief said, "You have disobeyed my words," and at once returned to her relatives in the deepest part of the river. The young husband, disconsolate, came daily and sat on a rock by the place where his wife had disappeared. One day the wife said to her father, "The grief of the orphan boy is great, shall I call him?" Her father said, "Let him come." So she spread her long hair all over the rock, and the next time her husband came he sat down on it, and she dragged him into the water. From that time on men have died by drowning.

Why the Kachins sacrifice to the nat (spirit) of jealousy. The Kachins have personified envy and jealousy more distinctly than any other human failing. They attribute almost every evil and misfortune to the jealous thoughts and intentions of someone who cannot bear to see their fortune or prosperity. The source of it all is traced to the following incident, reminding us of Cain and Abel. Long ago there were two brothers. The older was large in body, but the younger, while smaller in size, had the most active mind. When sowing-time came he said to his older brother, "Let us sow our fields." The older brother asked, "What shall we sow?" The younger brother in mischief said, "Sow your field with the scrapings of horns of cattle." Having given such advice he sowed his own with millet. The older brother in his innocence made scrapings from cattle's horns and sowed his field with it. After some time the older brother said to the younger, "What about your field?" The younger one said, "My field is full of sprouts, how about yours?" to which he received the reply, "My field is full of small cattle." When the younger brother realized that fortune had thus favored his weak-minded brother, he was full of envy, and taking some flour he painted all the cattle white and said, "The white ones belong to me." The older brother in anger caused a rain-storm to wash away the flour, and all returned to their natural colour except a few who ran under a big tree for shelter and became striped. The younger brother, far from satisfied with the outcome of his endeavor, devised a new stratagem to destroy the elder, and get possession of his herd. So he said, "Brother, your sister-in-law is dead, let us make her a coffin." This being done he said, "Now lie down in it and let us see if it is the right size." The elder brother doing so, the younger quickly put on the lid and secured it with strong rattan bands. But the strength of the older brother was sufficient to effect his release. Stepping out of the coffin he said to his younger brother, "Now you try it." The younger did not dare to disobey and the older at once tied down the lid with cords that could not be broken. Remembering his brother's endeavors to destroy him he took the coffin and hung it at a precipice just above a water-fall. After some time he said to the roaring stream, "Go and call the man that is hanging over the fall." The stream misunderstood the order, thinking he had been told to cut him down and acted accordingly. In Kachin there is a word-play impossible to reproduce: *sa gintan yu su,* go and call; *sa dan dat su,* go and cut down. Thus the younger brother (*N Naw*) died because of his jealousy and greed, and to this day the genius (*nat*) of jealousy generally called *Nsu nat,* is also called *Nnaw nat.* The meat of sacrifices offered to this nat is never given to children, so as to keep them from envy and a jealous disposition.

How paddy was obtained. Originally paddy was found only in the land of the sun. Then the children of men went and asked that they be given some, and their request was granted. On their return they were compelled to pass the house of the chameleon, the headman of *Kăang Shingra,* who had on former occasions shown his evil disposition. So they agreed to pass as quietly as possible, but the quick steps of the pony and the heavy foot-fall of the buffalo attracted his attention. "Where have you been," he asked, "and what are you carrying?" The men said, "We have been to the land of the sun, and are carrying back paddy." "Ah," he said, "and what has the Sun-*nat* decreed in regard to the size your paddy is to grow?" The reply came, "The stalks are to be the size of baffalo's legs, and the ears as long as a pony's tail." Hearing this the Chameleon said, "Not at all; it is quite enough if the ears are as large as my tail, and the stalks grow the size of my leg." Hence the Kachins have the proverb, *Shănyen a ga jăhten ai,* meaning that the words of the despisable chameleon nullified (lit. destroyed) the word of the mighty sun-*nat.*

How water was found. Formerly there was no water and human beings could not boil the rice and thus grew thin and weak. At that time there was a wise woman named *Sumbwi Nang Măjan.* She made a leech from one of her fingers and sent it on to the sky to fetch the water, but the leech never got that far and never found the water. Then the woman made an eagle from her lap, but while he soared over the highest mountains, he never reached

A hut in the rice field and pole with baskets containing offerings to *nats*.

P. 128.

the sky and failed to find the water. Then the woman made a yellow bee from one of her fingers, and the bee succeeded in reaching the sky and filled its mouth with water. Descending the bee rested on a cinnamon tree, and wishing to open its mouth the water ran out and emptied into the trunk of a hollow tree. Then the woman made a mole from her hand which worked into the tree and brought out the water in its mouth, but lost it all among some rocks, trying to pass over a very rocky place. Then the woman made a crab to find the water among the stones, but the crab said, "I must have a partner," and so she made a cicada. Then she gave instructions to both, saying to the crab, "If you are not back before July and August, the otter will devour you." To the cicada she said, "If you do not 'sing' here before the height of summer, the eagle will pick you up and eat you." Thus the cicada was heard during the time which now is the height of the rainy season by a spring outside a village, and the crab now brought the water to mankind. But the sons of men did not know how to appreciate the gift until they found that the animals of the jungle were depositing parts of it here and there near their dwelling places and planting trees around for shade. But from that time on the children of men have sacrificed to the spirit of the rivers and the springs.

CHAPTER XII.

IN QUEST OF THE UNKNOWN.

In Chapter XIII we intend to deal with the Kachin religion, but in order to understand the subject of the next paragraphs, it is necessary to say a few words regarding the fundamentals of their belief. Like all backward races, as well as orientals in general, they have a strong faith in the invisible and are extremely superstitious. Their faith centers around supernatural beings, called *nats,* who are superior to man but inferior to the gods of Greek or Indian mythology. These *nats* correspond more closely to our ideas of demons or evil spirits; still they are not all bad, and they are capable of good deeds as well as evil. The *nats* determine the destiny of men. Still there are with many a belief in fate, destiny (*auba*), in our sense of the word. But this idea comes from the Shan and Chinese. The *nats* follow man from birth to death as his shadow for good or for bad. They know all his ways and if disposed can reveal his future. It is this side of their faith that demands our attention in this chapter. In order to spy behind the veil of the future the Kachins have their mediums, diviners, divinations, palmists, sorcerers and interpreters of dreams, augeries and omens. Nothing is done without first consulting the spirits. There are rules and regulations for every important event and business transaction, and not to observe the regular customs may cause bad luck and bring disfavor from the nats.

The medium or nat-prophet (*myihtoi*). The chief oracle of the spirit world is the *nat*-prophet, or as he more correctly ought to be called, the medium. He resembles in almost every particular the medium who in a trance makes known the will of the spirits at a spiritualistic seance. His methods are practically the same, except that he does not need a dark room or closed doors. The results are identical. The medium may be a man, a woman or a child; he may or may not be a priest; his office is not strictly religious. Anyone suffering from epilepsy, nervous disorder or hysteria, is regarded as under the special power of the *nats,* and it is from these that the mediums mostly come. In connection with these natural tendencies, if the individual desires to profit from his powers, he will practice the usual arts belonging to this branch of the *nat*-worship, and will soon be able to place himself *en rapport* with the spirit world almost at will. For cash or other material considerations he will, when called upon, reveal the will of the *nats.* These prophets (lit. the men with the enlightened eye), are held in great respect and awe, and at death are not buried until the seventh day for fear that they are not really dead, but simply on a journey to the *nat*-country. They have as a rule a high "airy," reached by a tall bamboo ladder erected outside their abode, and in this they receive their inspiration; but they may get in touch with the *nats* anywhere and at any time. Extraordinary stories are afloat regarding the power and supernatural ability of the mediums, and some of them have been credited even by Europeans. We give here a graphic account by Dr. Anderson, as reprinted in "The Upper Burma Gazetteer," as it shows the *myihtoi* at his best, and how the performance was regarded by the observers. It took place when Colonel Sladen in 1868 was attempting to reach Momein via Bhamo and the Kachin hills.

"The *mi-tway* (*myihtoi*) now entered and seated himself on a small stool in one corner (of the house), which had been freshly sprinkled with water; he then blew through a small tube and, throwing it from him with a deep groan, at once fell into an extraordinary state of tremor: every limb quivered, and his feet beat a literal devil's tattoo on the bamboo flooring. He groaned as if in pain, tore his hair, passed his hands with maniacal gestures over his head and face, then broke into a short, wild chant, interrupted with sighs and groans, his features appearing distorted with madness or rage, while the tones of his voice changed to an expression of anger or fury. During this extraordinary scene, which realized all one had read of demoniacal possession, the *Sawbwa* (village chief) and his *pawmaings* (advisers) occasionally addressed him in low tones as if soothing him or deprecating the anger of the dominant spirit; and at last the *Sawbwa* informed Sladen that the *nats* must be appeased with an offering. Fifteen rupees and some cloth were produced: the silver on a bamboo sprinkled with water, and the cloth on a platter of plantain leaves were humbly laid at the diviner's feet, but with one convulsive jerk of the legs, rupees and cloth were instantly kicked away, and the medium by increased convulsions and groans intimated the dissatisfaction of the *nats* with the offerings. The *Sawbwa* in vain supplicated for its acceptance and then signified to Sladen that more rupees were required and mentioned sixty as the propitiatory sum. Sladen tendered five more with the assurance that no more could be given. The amended offering was again, but more gently pushed away, of which no notice was taken. After another quarter of an hour, during which the convulsions and groans gradually became less violent, a dried leaf rolled into a cone and filled with rice was handed over to the *mi-tway*. He raised it to his forehead several times and then threw it on the floor. A *da* (long knife) which had been carefully washed, was next handed over to him and treated in the same way; and after a few gentle sighs he rose from his seat and laughing, signed to us to look at his arms and legs, which were very tired. The oracle was in our favor, and predictions of all manner of success were interpreted to us as the utterance of the inspired diviner."

Dr. Anderson assures us as he continues his account, "It must not be supposed that this was a solemn farce enacted to conjure rupees out of European pockets. The *Kakhyens* (Kachins) never undertake any business or journey without consulting the will of the *nats* as revealed by a *mitway* under the influence of a temporary frenzy, or, as they deem it, possession." A more intimate knowledge of the Kachins would have modified these last statements. The medium is consulted only on more important occasions such as the one on hand. In some localities certain cheap prophets may be consulted about almost anything, but this is not the rule. It is strange, however, that so keen an observer as Dr. Anderson should have failed to see that most of this performance was nothing else but a "farce enacted to conjure rupees out of European pockets." The mere fact that twenty rupees were accepted when it became clear that sixty would not be given, would give the clue to this. The frenzy, the groaning and convulsions were all there, the prophet is an adept in this, but he was never so completely under the spell, but that he had a keen eye to business. Fifteen rupees is a princely sum for any prophet and under ordinary conditions he would have been satisfied with a fraction of this, but here was an expedition headed by Englishmen with an iron box full of silver. The propet correctly divined that a man who could afford to give fifteen rupees could give more, and hence the "kick." The *nats,* however, had to take it good naturedly, when they realized that the *Kala* (foreigner) would give only five more. This business instinct is quite characteristic of not only the mediums, but of other professional diviners. They always know about how much their clients are willing and able to pay, and they formulate their replies and requests accordingly.

Other stories regarding the wondrous things a medium can do when under the spell are quite numerous. He can cut his tongue and lips, and the blood will flow, but in an instant he is healed again when coming out of the trance. He can walk up a ladder "the steps of which consist of sword blades with the sharp edges turned upwards." I have never yet found a prophet willing to give an exhibition along these lines, even though I have offered substantial reward, provided I was allowed to closely examine the proceedings. The intimation always is that such inspection on my part would discourage the *nats*, which is no doubt true. Besides, I have never found a Kachin, who when closely questioned, could say that he has actually seen it himself. They all believe it has been done or can be done, just as a Shan or a Burman believes in invulnerability, even though they have never seen an invulnerable individual. Of course a small knowledge of legerdemain, or the art of the Indian juggler, can easily produce a bloodly tongue and mouth; and as for stepping on the edges of swords or sitting on bamboo spikes, it does not require a great deal of skill to deceive a crowd of unlookers who are not at all troubled with any "higher criticism" on the subject. A few have learned the simpler forms of jugglery from the Chinese, but the art is not extensively practiced.

The diviner (*ningwawt*). The diviner is more of a professional than the medium. He is very often a priest (*ningwawt-dumsa*), but not always. Divination is not confined to the religious sphere, and the diviner is primarily a man who ascertains the will and wishes of the spirits in anything that pertains to the affairs of the individual or the community. If he is also a priest his combined office gives him a great deal of power and influence. If, as is often the case, he is an old gray-haired man, both young and old stand in awe of him, as it is the belief that he is in especially close relation to the spirit-world. It need hardly be said that he has it in his power to interpret the will of his supernatural advisers much to his own advantage. He can always procure the kind of sacrifice that will give him the best return for his time and trouble. He can give anyone whom he dislikes an unpleasant time, as he can threaten all kinds of punishments from the spirits. Still it must not be thought that the diviner, any more than the medium, is altogether an impostor or a humbug. They believe in the spirit-world and in the activity of the *nats*. When their guesses and divinations come true, they always regard it as a direct favor from the spirits; when the opposite proves to be the case, they feel sure that some mistake has been made from their side, and thus the favor has been withheld. But being in possession of the power and influence their position secures them, it is only natural that they should use it somewhat to their personal advantage.

Divination. There is probably nothing in which our Kachins so firmly believe as in the efficacy of divination. If a child is born, a woman married or an individual buried; if a house is built or burned; a journey begun or a business transaction ended; if a person is ill, or has suffered misfortune; if the lightning has struck or a man-eating tiger is roaming about; in fact in almost any situation of importance it is necessary to call the diviner who by his art ascertains the will of the *nats*, the cause of the trouble and the sacrifice demanded. Divination is an important factor in the religious life of the community, but is capable of a wider application. If cattle have gone astray, their whereabouts may be determined by the use of the divining bamboo; if a thief or a witch is troubling the community, the easiest way to detect him may be by the art of divination. Lucky and unlucky days, the outcome of a hunt, a trading expedition, a raid or a venture in gambling, may be disclosed by consulting the *nats* by the help of the diviner.

There are numerous methods of divination. The Kachins have no objection to try the merits of any form or method that may come under their observation. Hence we find Chinese methods, such as the use of an egg, some kinds of plants and bones of fowls, in use among those who live near the Chinese frontier. In the Shan States leading Kachin diviners employ the magic square, rice and some cabalistic writings on palm leaves. The Atsis make use of thirty-three bamboo splints about the length of knitting needles, some of them carved at the top-end. These are

Priest divining with bamboo.

P. 136.

thrown up and tossed in such a way that they fall haphazard between the clefts of the fingers. The odd sticks in each group are picked out and laid aside. The process is repeated three times. If the result is an even number of sticks, the reply is favorable; if it is an odd number, it is unfavorable. Those who have learned to read Shan are guided by the Shan manuscripts on the subject. But these and similar methods are introduced from the outside. The genuine ways of Kachin divination are only three.

a. By the use of a stone attached to a string or shaken and held in certain positions in the hands. This according to tradition is the oldest form of divination, but it is today practiced or understood by only a few of the Northern Kachins.

b. By the use of a small bamboo called *shăman.* This is the most common and the most reliable way. The bamboo is praised and lauded, is called the Kachin book, the heavenly bamboo, the gift of the *nat* of wealth. The diviner sits on a low stool, and holding the bamboo over a slow fire he mutters a charm or incantation admonishing the bamboo not "to lie" or "mislead" those seeking information. Two of these bamboos are always carried at the same time; to carry only one indicates that he is about to measure a corpse for a coffin. The bamboo being held over the fire for a short while, it bursts joint by joint with a loud report, and from the position of the hairy fibres that stand out on each side of the fracture the will of the *nats* is interpreted. If the fibres stand out, crossing each other, it indicates that the *nats* desire a large offering on a cross. If they stand straight up, the meaning is doubtful and new experiments must be made. If leaning to one side or other, it means that eggs, fowls or pigs are desired. But there are many ways to interpret the position of these fibres, and it is left more or less to the fancy or usage of the particular diviner or locality.

c. By the *shăba lap.* This is a long leaf, resembling those of the cannæ, with sharp veins running parallel and not interlacing. The leaf is torn following the veins, and a number of shreds are thus produced which are taken haphazard, twisted and tied together. The diviner mutters his charms and prayers imploring the desired result. The knots and strands contained in each division are then counted and the outcome is determined from the number on each side and whether they are even or odd. Repeated trials are required, and this method is not as sure or effective as that with the divining bamboo.

Auguries. The belief in auguries is not as strong as in divination. It is resorted to only to a limited degree. The bones of the legs of fowls and the spleen of a hog, and in some localities the entrails of cattle, are used in forecasting the future. Some following a Chinese custom draw auguries from the head of a fowl killed in a certain way. At a wedding in the Gauri hills a young hen is taken to represent the bride. Some old man pronounces a charm, holding the hen before the elephant grass which the bride has passed. The hen is then let go. If it makes a bee-line for the house it is considered a good sign, the bride will be a home-maker and bring prosperity. If the hen starts off for the jungle, it is a sign that she will draw away from the home, squander rather than gather. I have not seen this custom followed in other parts of the country, but it may be. The calling of the owl near a house is a bad sign, and the falling of a large tree indicates the death of some leading man. But there is a great diversity in regard to these things, and in each community there may be some particular kind of belief belonging only to that locality.

Omens. There are two kinds of omens. Those called *numdaw numdaw,* meaning animals crossing one's path, (lit. impeding one's progress). Merely to see an animal by the roadside has no meaning, but if certain kinds cross the path it has its significance. The other kind is drawn from the calling of birds or beasts and from almost anything out of the ordinary. If a snake, porcupine or wild cat crosses one's path, some of your friends will die, or your undertaking will not prosper. If a deer, hedgehog or rhinoceros crosses the path, it is a good omen, luck is on your side. The only exception is the barking deer; if one of those run across, bad reports will follow. If you see weasels playing or fighting, it is a bad sign; they will entice the human spirit to stray and wander. If two barking deer call at the same time outside a village, illness or fire will follow. If young cattle stray into a house, or go up the roof, the *nats* are after them and they are destined soon to be sacrificed, which means that illness will visit the house. A ring around the sun signifies the death of a chief. Crows calling in a peculiar way outside a house bring messages from friends just deceased. Hence there is a proverb, "He does not even utter the sound of the crow," which means that an old friend has so completely forgotten his former associates that he never sends them any message or token of regard. If the steps of a jungle animal are seen around a newly dug grave, some relatives will soon follow. Thus the immediate surroundings of a grave are carefully inspected the morning after burial. If the boiling rice "breaks" in the pot and does not adhere in one lump, some accident will happen to someone in the house. If soot falls from the roof into food that is being prepared, it is a bad sign. If rats build nests in a grave, the relatives of the interred will be poor. These are a few of the bad omens; the good, which are few, are hardly ever mentioned.

Dreams. Primitive man has always paid a great deal of attention to dreams. The Kachins are no exception. The meaning is sought of almost every dream, and most of the older men know the rules regulating their interpretation. The following is some of the wisdom along this line. To dream about a broken tree, the setting sun or moon, is unfortunate; it presages a speedy death. To dream that young fowls on the back porch are scattered is bad, to dream that they are gathered is good, A dream about the horn-bill is a presentiment of power and influence. A dream about large cattle is good; the spirits are replenishing your stables. To dream about slaves, trade, fruit, a flowering tree, growing bamboo, a heap of stone or a herd of hogs, indicates that your family will increase and that fortune is yours. To see in the visions of the night an old paddy house, or a swarm of bees at the top of your house is a good morning dream, you will have abundance. Apparently the Kachin interpreter of dreams is not inclined to think that these things always go by opposites.

Charms. All the races and tribes of Burma are firm believers in the protecting power of charms, and most men always have with them at least some object to ward off danger. All over Burma can be found implements from the stone and bronze age, and these are universally believed to be "thunder-bolts," and are kept in the houses to ward off fire. In case of complications at child-birth, by placing a stone-knife or arrow-head on the top of the head of the labouring woman all difficulties will disappear. This belief in the reality of the "thunder-bolt" and its power and efficacy is very common, even among highly intelligent natives. Precious stones, tusks of the wild boar, and pieces of charmed metals inserted under the skin are very desirable objects in time of war. A powerful charm, obtained from a certain kind of bird, the skull of a killed man or the hand of an abortion, called *wam,* will make a man invisible. Tattooing to secure invulnerability has been introduced by the Shans. Many of the Kachin chiefs and leading men living in the Northern Shan States have been tattooed with the magic square on their backs, and other cabalistic figures on shoulders and arms. The fact that these bear Buddhist inscriptions does not make any difference to the *nat*-worshipping Kachins. By the help of the *nats* an evil disposed person can send a missile, called *lawng,* in the form of a knife, needle, bone, piece of leather or the like, right into the heart or the liver of an enemy, and special charms are worn to ward off such danger. The tusk of the wild-boar, which will grow after the animal is dead, and the jaw-bone of a tiger, are regarded as especially helpful when hunting, or when traveling in wild jungle. As with the Burmans and Shans, so the Kachins firmly believe in the power of these charms, even though they see them fail over and over again. That there is some way of securing complete protection from physical violence they never doubt, and the necromancer's assistance is eagerly sought.

Rules to insure good luck. Good or bad luck accounts for nearly everything in the small affairs of everyday life, and luck has something to do with the *nats,* or the mysterious something that like a shadow always follows human beings. There are rules to be observed in almost everything pertaining to commerce, industry, and the social side of life. Every community has some particular reason for some custom or observance, probably not recognized anywhere else, and thus such rules become too numerous to be mentioned in detail. It is enough to indicate the general trend, which is the same everywhere. A hunter looking for game must not speak to anyone that he may meet. Should he disclose his purpose he is sure to be unsuccessful. He will also be guided by the omens mentioned above. Returning with a bag the village priest *hkinjawng* cuts off the part of the flesh intended for the *nats,* and an offering is presented at the altar of the house-*nats.* In some localities certain kinds of plants are blessed and kept as a charm (*shan tsi,*) to facinate and entice the game of the jungle. Where this is the case the hunter must sprinkle some of the blood toward the plant in order to propitiate the genius of the hunt. If there is a chase, and the whole village is concerned, it must first be ascertained by divination if the day is propitious and the *nats* are in favor. Some guns, traps or snares are more "lucky" than others. The "spirit," genius or "life" of a good gun (*sămyeng*) is sometimes seen "playing" or "dancing" on the gun; this is always a good sign and such a weapon is sure to kill. If a gun, trap or snare be handled in a way displeasing to the *nats,* luck is gone and nothing will be hit or caught. In fishing very much the same rules are observed. Not to speak to anyone on the road, not to expect too much, and even if there is a good haul to speak of it in a deprecating manner, are important rules to observe.

Everyday life is hedged about with similar customs and observances. A person must not crawl under the bars at the stable entrance. He must not crawl under a house, as there may be women in the house, and it is very unfortunate if a man at any moment finds himself at a lower elevation than a woman. To dress a man in a woman's skirt is not only dishonoring him, it will make him unlucky. No one must step over a person asleep or when simply reclining, and a woman must never step across the rope or a pole that may happen to be in her way. She must remove it or pass under it. A Kachin does not wish to have anything said in regard to possible misfortune and death. A malicious, or even a playful insinuation or suggestion is deeply resented. It establishes what he calls an *ana akra,* an unpleasant foreboding, or an invisible "brand" which before the *nats* may mark him as a doomed man.

The number nine is the sacred number in Kachin lore, but otherwise it does not have any particular significance. There is no especial meaning attached to it in regard to life nowadays. Only formerly everything revolved around the number nine.

Ordeals. It is quite natural that to a people so full of superstition, the ancient custom of appealing to ordeals should not be unknown. Some of the most common forms are the following. An accused party may prove the falsity of the charge by dipping the hand into boiling water or melting lead. If no harm comes to the person on trial innocence is established. Nowadays this severe test is (wisely) never resorted to, and milder forms are taking its place. An egg is broken, and the defendant dips the end of a stalk of elephant grass into the yolk; if any of the yellow adheres to the grass he is guilty, if not he is innocent.

Formerly a common test was to invoke the lightning to strike one dead if guilty. The village priest conducted the proceedings. The contending parties sat facing each other, each with a long pole in his hand. The priest reciting his incantations implored the *nat* of thunder to indicate the guilty. As he finished, the lightning, it may be from a perfectly clear sky, would strike and kill the offender on the spot. No one nowadays pretends to be able to work this miracle.

The water-test is, however, still practiced. The accused and his friends stand on one side of a river, and the accuser and his party stand on the opposite. Cattle, money or household goods are brought forth, and in the presence of witnesses it is agreed that if the accused is proved innocent his accusers must deliver all they have brought to him, if the opposite proves to be the case he must lose all on his side. After due ceremonies of the priest, the chief parties from both sides go down into the stream. The guilty party finds it impossible to put his head under the water, while he does it with ease if innocent. This would seem to be a particularly easy test, provided the guilty party did not allow his imagination to run away with him. Other forms borrowed from Shans and Burmans are also resorted to, but this kind of trial is getting more and more uncommon, as the people have more confidence in British justice than in the impartiality of the *nats*.

Witch-craft. The belief in witches and wizards is common all over Burma, and has been recognized by law and custom. From a Kachin point of view a witch is a person "with two souls," one his own and the other belonging to a *nat*. The individual may or may not be conscious of the fact. He has the power to "harm others by an occult influence," but it is not necessary that he should be aware that he is thus bent on mischief. This is discovered by the rules of divination, and the witch (it may be an individual or a whole family) never knows that he was taken possession of by a witch-*nat* until informed by the diviner. Two kinds of witch-spirits are recognized: the *lămum,* which is comparatively harmless, causing sores or minor troubles, and the *yu* (the rat) which in the shape of a rat enters and "eats out the inside" of a man. Convulsions, festering sores, misfortunes to cattle and horses are usually attributed to the *yu.*

When a person has been taken suddenly ill, and by divination it has become clear that a witch is at work, the first step is to find out the guilty party. This can as a rule be revealed only by the bewitched person himself. The spirit that has made him ill will through him make known what individual he belongs to. That individual may be a most unwilling party to the work he is doing. Sometimes it takes a great deal of coaxing and arguing with many threats or promises, to induce the spirit to reveal its identity. Promises are made, that "if you reveal yourself no harm will be done to the person you belong to;" "you will receive any gift you ask for;" "all we want is to know who you are, what you desire and your every wish will be granted," and more to that effect. When, however, their object is gained, a different tale will be told. The unfortunate party or family may be driven away from home and village or sold into slavery. It is easy to see how this superstition would in the hands of unscrupulous persons be a powerful weapon against anyone toward whom they held a grudge. He could accuse anyone and there was really no way to prove that he was wrong. A man of influence, backed up by the priests and other leading men, could accuse anyone he pleased and he would be disposed of as just described or even killed. A large number of the slaves all over the Hills are such unfortunate men and women who have been charged with being possessed by these troublesome spirits.

Black cats, if found in witch-families, are said to have the

Priest beseeching the *nats*. P. 144.

power to cause the death of rats or fowls by merely looking at them. If such a cat jumps over a corpse lying in state, it will cause the spirit of the dead person to wander and stray from the road it ought to take. If an individual, or a family become convinced that they are really the mediums through which the spirits do their mischief, they may make a public confession and at a sacrifice make a promise that in case it again becomes clear that the witch-spirits through them are doing harm, they will agree to be sold into slavery, or even to be punished with death. This is intended more as a warning to the spirit than to its unwilling human instrument. There are no remedies known for witches. Some carry charms to protect them against this evil, but no one can be sure. Some bewitch by merely looking at a person. This reminds us of the "evil eye," and children are especially susceptible to this influence. Many of the trinkets or plugged coins worn by children are really charms to guard against this form of evil. In olden time if an individual died, being "bewitched," his family or tribe would often apply the "lynch law," and either kill or enslave the family without any further consultation with chiefs and elders. Many of the Kachins cannot understand why the British law protects witches, and why they are not allowed to dispose of them according to old customs and traditions. With them there is no doubt that the danger is real, and they fully believe that only the most drastic measures will be of any use.

Cursing, (*mătsa dat ai*). If an unpardonable offence has been committed and the guilty party refuses to submit to a fine or settlement on fair terms, the sufferer may resort to the expedient of "sending a curse," by which with the help of the *nats* the offender will suffer bodily affliction and even death.

The *sa hye măraw,* the "fate causing dysentery," is the evil genius usually invoked and sent on the mission of cursing and punishing the intended victim. A priest familiar with the "service" of this *nat* is called and in the deepest secrecy he with the instigator plans the details. The priest receives a handsome present if his curse is effective, at all events he is given a sword or a spear. It is important that the victim should know nothing about what is going on, as the curse may be ineffective and a heavy fine will be imposed upon the "curser" if anything leaks out.

By divination it is ascertained what kind of an offering is required. It must be either a dog, a hog or a goat. Besides, as supplementary offerings are provided (1) seven bamboo sections filled with soil from the stable; (2) a very offensive smelling kind of fruit; (3) wild ginger and dried fish, and (4) a species of ground-rat (*măgan*). These are made up into seven packages, placed in seven bamboos, rolled in seven plantain leaves. Seven stalks of tall elephant grass and seven stalks of a large reed are pointed and placed with the offerings.

The imprecation always takes place at evening, and in order that no one may suspect the real nature of the proceedings it is intimated that he is expelling the *nat* of malediction from his own house. When the priest is done with the preliminaries and has recited his formulas of "cursing," the "imprecator," the priest, and five or six trusted companions, go out on the road leading to the victim's house or village. There they select a cinnamon tree and to this is tied the main sacrifice. The supplementary offerings are tied around the trunk of the tree. The priest begins the imprecations proper, invoking all kinds of calamaties to visit the victim. During this he holds a stalk of the reed and elephant grass in his hand balancing them like a spear. Finishing the list of his curses he throws the "spear," aiming at the offerings tied to the tree. If it hits and remains right in the center of one of them, it is a sure sign that the curse is effective. The priest having thrown his spear, others present do the same, and each is aimed at the heart of the enemy. If guns are used the tree is riddled with bullets. When all is ended and the party is ready to return, the sacrifice (usually a dog) is killed, and either buried at the place or hung up near the tree, as indicated by the diviner.

In regard to all these ways of looking into the future it is interesting to notice how similar practices are found among all the related tribes and races of eastern Asia. It is impossible to claim originality for any one tribe or people. It all belongs to the common deposit, and beliefs, rules and customs have found their way from north to south, from east to west, only being modified as they have been adopted by one tribe or another. There is no absolute uniformity in customs even among the same clan or family. In the case of witchcraft, for instance, some Kachins follow a practice which may in reality be Shan or Burmese. When the witch has made known its identity, and told (of course through the afflicted person), what "presents" are required, these are placed in a basket and carried outside. If the spirit is satisfied, the afflicted party will at once "feel better," and gradually improve as the witch-spirit has taken its departure. If on the other hand the party grows worse, other measures must be resorted to. A sacrifice may be offered in the jungle in which the people of the house must not partake, and other offerings may be made as directed by divination.

Magic, in the proper sense of the word, is not an important part. Magicians are few, and those who know how to practice the "black art" are still fewer. The belief is growing that in these degenerate days, when books and the ways of the *kala* take the place of the ancestral "wisdom," these secrets are rapidly being forgotten, and the supernatural powers who assisted in all these things are not able to show their particular abilities as they did formerly. It is the complaint of the negro preacher over again, that too many questions spoil all our theology.

CHAPTER XIII.

THE KACHIN RELIGION.

We have already mentioned that the religion common to all the Kachin tribes is spirit worship or demonolatry. It is Shamanism or animism in a form peculiarily adapted to the habits and intellectual development of a semi-savage mountain people. The term *nat*-worship generally employed in Burma, defines more clearly than any other the special form of animism common to the whole of eastern Asia. All the Mongolian tribes and races are at heart animists, whatever form of religion they may otherwise profess. A Chinaman or a Burman is as truely a spirit worshipper as a Chin or a Kachin. Rituals, ceremonies, creeds and forms of expression will differ, but back of it all lingers the primitive faith in spirits, demons, *nats,* or whatever they may be called. The great ethnic religions of Asia have never been able to eradicate the deep-rooted belief among the masses, that ghosts, spirits, demons, angels or devils, are able to interfere in the affairs of men. All over India and in Mohammedan countries nothing is more in evidence than the shrine to some departed saint, some guardian spirit, or miniature god or goddess of hardly more than local importance. Even in Europe some of these forms of superstition are still in evidence among the less educated. In the Kachin Hills we can still read the ancestral story, in nearly its original form, of many a tribe and race that has advanced to a higher form of faith. It is from this point of view that the religion of backward races is of especial importance to the student of religious evolution. But apart from this, if we wish to understand the heart and mind of a savage tribe, we must know their forms of worship and their religious fears and hopes. The savage is far more religious than his civilized brother. Religion is of the very first importance to him. Everything he does can be traced to some form of belief, to some religious custom and superstition. His whole social and family life is regulated by his religious practices, and in his work or amusement he is always under the shadow of his invisible guardians or tormentors. They follow him as his own shadow from the cradle to the grave.

It is difficult to induce a Kachin to reveal the mysteries of his faith. From a secret dread of the *nats* he will keep back, even when closely questioned, the most interesting and important details. Besides, the ordinary Kachin is no more familiar with the intricacies of his elaborate ritual than are the uninitiated with the particulars belonging to higher forms of faith. He follows the leadership of the priests, and those that attend to the sacrificial service. It is enough for him to observe the rules and regulations elaborated by custom and usage from ancestral times. The hill tribes have for centuries been in contact with the great oriental religions; but neither Buddhism, Confucianism nor Hinduism have attracted or influenced them in any important particulars. A few have accepted a degenerate form of Shan Buddhism, and some Chinese customs are traceable here and there, but the great mass of our illiterate mountaineers hold the ancestral faith, and sacrifice to the spirits.

Back of the spirit worship in its most developed forms we find *ancestor worship,* nekrolatry, the fear of the departed, the awe in the presence of death. Among the Chinese and Japanese we meet this faith in its most advanced stage; among semi-savages it retains the primitive features. Even the higher *nats* were once nothing but ordinary mortals; but passing out from the mundane sphere they became invested with supernatural powers, and thus became the objects of fear, reverence and worship. To propitiate and appease such "shades," who as a rule exhibit a jealous and vindictive disposition, is the great objective in the Kachin ritual. How to do it is his one absorbing question.

These spirits, demons, shades or *nats*, are innumerable and occupy every imaginable place above and below. They rule the sun, the moon and the sky. They dwell on every mountain top, in every spring, lake or stream. Every waterfall, cave or precipitous rock will have its guardian, as well as every wood, field or large tree. Each village, tribe or family, may have their particular divinities to whom special attention is due. The supernatural intruders have nothing in common with the old classic gods or goddesses, and only a distant relationship with the fairies, fates, kobolds, trolls and hobgoblins of mediaeval Europe. The delightful inhabitants of Teutonic or Scandinavian fairy-land, or the sylvan denizens that entertain us in "A Midsummer Night's Dream," do not thrive in the forests and bamboo groves of the Kachin hills.

The Kachins live in constant dread of the *nats*, who are always ready to take revenge if trespasses, knowingly or unknowingly, are committed. If the usual sacrifices are withheld; if a vessel, shrine or altar belonging to the sacrificial service has been desecrated; if anyone has stepped into the place set apart for the guardian household *nats*, or if without any apparant reason whatsoever a spirit capriciously desires a fresh offering, some misfortune will befall the unfortunate individual, family or community. Houses will burn, fields be devastated, the crops will fail, bad luck will follow every undertaking, illness or epidemics will visit men and beasts, and misery, poverty and death will follow. The *nats* alone can re-establish fortune and happiness and in the case of disease administer the remedies; but not being of a compassionate nature, they never render assistance unless properly propitiated. Thus the life of a Kachin is one long struggle against adverse powers, one continuous effort to keep on the good side of the always troublesome *nats*.

There is no clear trace of totemism among the Kachins. The fact that there is a prescribed form of names for all the children does not indicate any belief in a family or tribal totem. The explanation of this custom has already been given; in these names are perpetuated the names of the primitive spirits, but these cannot be called totems. Of a primitive fetichism there are only very faint indications. The use of charms and amulets goes back to ancestral times; but the objects now used are mostly obtained from the Shans and Chinese. Tatooing is a late introduction from the Shan, and those who live away from Shan communities hardly ever submit to the practice. Trees, rocks or animals are never worshipped even though they may be regarded as inhabited by *nats,* and no images of any kind are ever made or used.

The priesthood. In every village are found certain individuals attending to the religious need of the community. They are as a rule the most intelligent and best informed, but are not distinguished by dress, habits or morals. There is no ecclesiastical organization, but certain grades are recognized, and the duties of each are clearly defined. The priest alone is familiar with the religious language chanted at the sacrificial service. There are special formulas, addressing the different orders of *nats,* celestial, terrestrial and ancestral, and only the initiated are familiar with contents and phraseology. The priest is generally a leading diviner, who by his art ascertains what *nat* is in evidence and what offering is required.

The highest religious authority is the *Jaiwa,* a kind of high-priest, who officiates on special occasions. He is usually an old, gray-haired man. He is familiar with everything concerning history, tradition and religion. At a great wedding or at the religious dance (*mănau*), he rehearses the whole Kachin history, from creation to our own times, taking three days and nights for this really marvellous feat of memory. It is all recited in rhythmic language, abounding, as do all the religious formulas, in parallelism and alliterations. He is supposed never to make a mistake as to form and substance, but the vocabulary and phraseology are left to a large extent to the choice of the individual. It is

Priest imploring *nats*.

P. 152.

a mistake to think that the long and tiresome rhapsodies recited on such occasions are all a meaningless jargon. A large part of the vocabulary is antiquated, or echoes reminiscences from an earlier past, but it is understood by "the elders" and is used among them in general conversation. Women and children may know very little of what is said, but all have a general idea as to meaning and importance. Anyone wishing to become a *Jaiwa*, or a priest, must learn the formulas and pay the price for instruction. The *Jaiwa* is liberally paid for his services, usually with cattle and gongs.

Next to the *Jaiwa* comes the regular priest (*dumsa*). Three grades may be recognized: those who can pronounce a blessing on ordinary occasions; those authorized to sacrifice to the ancestral spirits (*tsu dumsa*); and those who minister to the terrestrial and celestial *nats* (*ga dumsa*). The first class can offer only water, liquor, eggs and dried fish; the second class can in addition to these offer fowls and pigs, while the third reaches the height of sacrificing cattle, particularly buffaloes. Ordinarily the priest officiates in his everyday garb, but when addressing the *Mu* (celestial) *nat* he may put on something of a robe or gown, waving before him a bunch of tall elephant grass; and when the *nat* of wealth (*mădai*) is invoked, he wears a mitre ornamented with feathers, tusks and sometimes flowers. A part of the hind-quarter of the animal sacrificed goes to the priest for his services.

As a subordinate and assistant to the priest comes the *hkinjawng*, who officiates at the putting up of the altar, and cutting up of the sacrifice. If fowls are offered he hangs them at the alter in small baskets, and after the blessing is pronouned kills them by strangling. When larger sacrifices are on the programme he selects and arranges such parts as are intended for the *nats*, and presents the partakers with their portions. There is in connection with this a most minute and elaborate ritual that must be seen to be understood. The arranging of the leaves used for wrapping purposes, and the kind of meat to be placed on each has been developed into a fine art. He takes a small piece of each part of the sacrifice (a piece of thigh, shoulder, heart, liver, kidney etc.,) and wraps them up in small packages and presents them on the *nat*-altar. This functionary is paid with a part of the neck if it is a large offering, and a leg if it is a fowl.

As an assistant to the *hkinjawng* comes the *hpunglum,* who may be either a man or a woman. But on important occasions, when offerings are made to the celestial *nats,* (*mu, sinlap, bunghpoi* or *mădai*), only men are admitted. It then becomes his duty to kill (usually to spear) the sacrifice. In addition the *hpunglum* attends to the pouring of the libations, keeps the kettles boiling, and in general does the menial work of the occasion.

The medium (prophet) and diviner mentioned in the previous chapter may or may not officiate in a religious capacity. Their work is not confined to the religious sphere. Divination is always an important part in every case when offerings are made; but this may, and generally is, attended to by the priests.

Offerings. The Kachin *nats* are not over particular as to what is offered, and there is no distinction between clean and unclean animals. Thus may be presented water, liquor, rice, vegetables, rats, moles, squirrels, dried or fresh fish, prawns, eggs, fowls, pigs, cows and buffaloes. Goats and dogs are offered to the *nat* of insanity and the "fates" of accident. Dogs are generally offered in the Hokung valley where ordinarily would be presented fowls or small pigs, and in some localities "the barker" is killed to keep away the *nat* causing death in confinement (*sawn*) and the cruel genius of solitary places (*Jăhtung*). All smaller offerings are given whole, wrapped up in leaves and hung or placed on the shrine or altar, or placed in appropriate places in the house, as occasion demands. Water and liquor are presented in bamboo sections; eggs are strung up on bamboo splits and are seen hanging anywhere about the house, but especially near the front door, where they are presented to the *nat* causing sores, and at the back corner where the family altar is. When hogs or cattle are sacrificed, only a very small portion goes to the *nats*. The individual sacrificing, the chief and the priests, appropriate the most desirable portions, and the whole village has a feast. The *nat* in question is supposed to be satisfied with the "life," which is housed and kept "a hundred years" in the celestial stables. We have already mentioned the tradition regarding the "fruit of life." Another version has it that when men became mortal, having displeased the sun-*nats*, the domestic animals entered the garden by the side of the house of the first men. There the fowls ate the fruit of the plant of life, the cattle devoured the leaves and the hogs went for the roots. Thus the plant was killed and men complained. The guilty parties then promised that as they had destroyed the health and life-giving plant they would submit to become substitutes for man, giving up their lives for his. This tradition is always recited as an excuse for taking an innocent animal life whenever cattle are sacrificed.

Nat-altars. We have in Chapter III given a general idea of the places sacred to the *nats*, and mentioned the shrines or altars used as receptacles for the offerings. It is difficult to describe these altars as they bear no resemblance to anything we give this name. They are rather small tables or shelves, made in a rude and crude way of wood and bamboo. Taking the altar of the *nat* of heaven (*mu*) as a sample, we begin with a small log freshly cut from the jungle; this, having the length of eight or nine feet, is split about two-thirds down into four parts that are bent outward for the support of a wicker shelf or table about a foot and a half square. Small bunches of elephant grass are tied to the corners of this shelf and the whole is raised and fixed in the ground. There the altar remains until it falls down by decay, or is run down by cattle. The shapes and make-up of the different altars vary somewhat, but the general outlines are the same. A few altars resemble long settees, and some are more like a chair, thus somewhat resembling a shrine. But the only real shrine is put up to a *nat* called *Sămyin* introduced from the Shan. The crosses to which cattle are tied when sacrificed are made up of two heavy pieces of timber, fixed in the ground and tied together so as to form a St. Andrew's cross. Sometimes two heavy logs from trees just felled, fixed securely into the ground, serve the same purpose. The sacrifice is not hung up on the cross, but only tied to it while killed. The head or the skull alone is hung up on one of the posts.

The Nats. The number of *nats,* as already mentioned, is legion. They have existed from the earliest dawn of day, and still continue to multiply. No attempt is made to classify the innumerable inhabitants of the invisible world, but it is easy to trace several orders and degrees.

First come the primitive *nats* born of *Kringkrawn* and *Kringnawn,* who themselves are the children of wind and clouds. The names of these *nats,* seven in number, indicate their station, order of birth and work. These are:

La N-Gam, the first-born, the glorious chief, (*Jăhtung*).

La N-Naw, the celestial *Sinlap,* the flower of gold.

La N-La, the protector of the fields, the common laborer.

La N-Tu, the origin of strength and the strong arm.

La Ntang, the Lord of the sun.

La N-Yaw, the *nat* of wealth (*mădai*), the father of the Fates (*măraw*).

La N-Hka, the glorious light, the source of wisdom.

These primeval spirits have all passed away, but their names were transmitted to the first male children born of men, and are today carried by the sons in every family. Their work is carried on by their numerous children and descendants. We here meet with an early attempt of primitive man to personify the forces of nature.

The pair produced by wind and clouds, having in eight successive births given existence to the primeval spirits and the world in its chaotic state, there now appeared a mysterious couple *Chyănun* and *Woishun*. They gave birth to the celestial *nats* (*mătsaw ntsang ni*), the earth-spirits (*ga nat, shădip*), with which they are especially identified, and two orders of the Fates. These spirits are very closely connected with mundane affairs and human happiness. It is the spirit of the upper regions that speaks to us in the voice of the thunder, and the earth spirit can bless or undo every undertaking. In close relationship to these, while operating in a more limited sphere, are such spirits or demons as *Jăhtung*, a cruel monster inhabiting caves, waterfalls and dence forests; *Chyăga*, the cause of sores and skin diseases; *Sutnam*, a gnome or female hobgoblin, a single hair of which insures wealth and power. In many localities the *Sutnam* is identified with a "wild man of the woods" called *Chyăwoi*. This monster has only one eye in the middle of the forehead; the nose grows "up side down," the breasts reach to the ankles, and the heels "grow in front." Sometimes this strange individual appears in visible form, and anyone seeing the "man" will die at once. Lately, it is said, a woman saw one in a village near the Chinese frontier, and she died the same evening. We are here at a stage when the forces of nature take on more clearly defined types in the process of personification. As though the Kachin pantheon was not sufficient for all ordinary purposes, they have introduced the *Săgya* (*Thagya*) from the Burmese, and in the Northern Shan States many of the chiefs build small shrines to the Shan *nat*, *Sămyin*, who has the same unsavory reputation as the Kachin *Jăhtung*.

But the belief in the ancestral spirits, (*tsu nat*), has undoubtedly the strongest hold on the popular imagination. The belief in and reverence for these "shades" is the foundation of all forms of animism. Every individual at death becomes a *tsu*, a kind of half *nat* (compare the Egyptian *ka*), and in the final obsequies is sent off to the ancestral regions. If the *tsu* remains, nothing more is thought of it, but if determined to return, there is an additional *nat* to deal with. Most of the household *nats* (*gumgun gumhpai ni*), can trace their pedigree to some venerated father or mother, or some far away ancestor, who for some reason or other preferred the former habitation to the land of the departed. Strange to say returning spirits are nearly always bent on mischief. The affectionate mother will return from spirit land and in the shape of a chirping cricket entice the ghost of the still living child to wander away, and death will follow in a few months. A departed friend will return and leave his fingermarks on the boiling rice with the result that most of the partakers will sicken and die. An old respected chief, if not properly buried, will cause a drought or deluge, destroying the crops of the whole community. There is apparently no case on record where a departed spirit has improved in company with the shades.

In a class by themselves come the Fates (*măraw ni*), thirty-nine in number, probably distant relatives of the thirty-seven *nats* of the Burmese. They trace their ancestry to *La N-Yaw,* the sixth born of the primeval *nats.* They are especially jealous and revengeful, and their particular vocation is to observe and punish anything arousing pride, jealousy or contempt. We have here a personification of suspicion, envy and revenge. They notice all reports, good or bad; they listen to all slander, bad wishes, curses or ill-timed boasting; they record all undertakings and follow every individual from birth to death. The Kachin faith is: Speak about, think about, or do anything to arouse the "demon" and he is right there. Consequently whatever is done it is of the utmost importance that fate should be propitiated and harm averted. There is probably nothing that has a stronger hold than fear of the Fates, and nothing so dangerous to speak about. Five of the family are especially feared, viz., *Sin chyăwoi Janja doi,* the fate of darkness, the mother of them all and the most difficult to propitiate; *Nhtum du, Sa wa kănu,* the "mother of accidents; *Sa wa nu, Sa hti du,* the mother of accidents, and the Lord of the expiring breath; *Hku mădraw, Ra n-hkaw,* the fate of friendship, whose jealousy is proverbial, and *Nga li du, Nga htung kănu,* the dryad of the plantain groves, who knows all that happens on the road. The Fates most commonly propitiated are the *Kăjai mădraw,* the fate of current reports, the genius of aspersion or defamation, and the *Mătsa mădraw,* the demon of curses and maledictions. Hunting, fishing, working the fields or trading, at a funeral, housebuilding or a wedding, the *Kăjai mădraw,* the "genius of aspersion," is prominently before the minds of the individual or the community. At a wedding, for example, there must be offerings to the genius of the bride's family (*măyu mădraw*), to the husband's family (*mădu mădraw*), and the guiding spirit of the go-betweens (*kăsa mădraw*), must not be forgotten. But they all belong to the order of the *Kăjai mădraw.*

The exorcising of witches and witch-spirits has a religious side to it; otherwise the belief in witches in not necessarily a part of their religion. Consequently we have preferred to deal with the question of witches and witchcraft in the previous chapter. The witch spirit is an evil *nat* and must be treated accordingly; but most communities nowadays are not troubled by this misfortune as formerly. The fact that witches can no longer be sold or killed has a great deal to do with this.

The Kachins make it a point effectually to guard village and home by the help of the *nats.* At the village entrance is the place dedicated to the *nats* of the chief. In front of every house are numerous altars representative of offerings to various spirits from above and below. At the front door are emblems to the spirits causing skin diseases and other bodily afflictions, as they wish to be spared such visitations. At the back corner is the place for the household *nats,* the especial guardians of the family. By the sides and often at the back of the house are numerous crosses indicating the number of cattle slain. Their skulls are left on the cross or else hung as ornaments on the front post and wall. That this rather elaborate and costly system is a heavy drain on a people comparatively poor is selfevident. They themselves admit that their religion keeps them poor. They profess no love or real reverence for the *nats;* it is fear of the invisible *nats,* and a dread of the consequences of neglecting them, that is at the bottom of all their religious doings.

Propitiation of the nats. The aim and purpose of the Kachin spirit worship, is not greatly different from the objects sought by religious observances of mankind in all stages of civilization. The great objectives are to appease offended spirits, to secure protection, to obtain riches and prosperity, and to find relief in case of illness. The *nats* are the guardians of life, property and destiny, and their good will and favor are essential to health, prosperity and happiness.

When an individual, family or community suspects, or has become convinced, that their misfortune is due to the agency of the *nats,* the diviner is called, and the special *nat* in question is found. The offering required is ascertained and preparations are made accordingly. If the sacrifice demanded is not obtainable, or is above the means of the party for the time being, a promise is made that the offering will be forthcoming as early as possible, and a token to that effect, usually a small parcel containing some meat tied to a bamboo hoop, is placed in some appropriate place. When the day of the offering has arrived, the "altar" is made, the sacrifice is brought forth, the kettles are set boiling, and the priest begins his long monotonous recitals, that often keep him busy the whole day. Ritual and formula will vary as one or the other *nat* is addressed, but the usual order is as follows:

(1) Praise to the *nat,* extolling his greatness, ability to help and willingness to hear: he is told that he is able to "create a hundred blessings and grant a hundred gifts;" that, "Dancing on the sword's edge he is not hurt, walking

Hkinjawng or sacrificial *nat*-priest. P. 160.

on a cotton thread he does not fall," and more to the same effect.

(2) Reply by the *nat*, making known his abode, his demands and general interest in the case. He may tell the priest: "I take perfect care of golden youth, I guard the golden maidenhood," and that those who call on him "reach the summit of wealth and attain the height of riches;" that he is "the shade during the hot weather, and the protecting cave during the rainy season," and so on.

(3) Statement of the case, help desired for whom or what; the *nat* is implored to help the suffering, and no longer torment and oppress.

(4) The *nat* asking particulars as to offering, altar, priest, place and time, is assured that everything is the very best and that ancestral customs, rules and regulations are rigidly observed.

(5) Sacrifice promised, time, place and other particulars stated.

(6) The slaying of the sacrifice and distribution of the different kinds of meat; it is here that the *hkinjawng* and *hpunglum* are mostly in evidence.

(7) Exhorting the *nat* to accept the offering, remove the trouble and return to the heavenly abode, there to keep the "life" of the sacrifice and during that time hold his protecting hand over the worshippers:

Arise from the celestial table,
Remove from the heavenly altar,
Go back to the glorious heights,
Return to the celestial abode.
Do not revert from the path,
Do not turn aside from the road.
Remain in the celestial heights,
Abide in thy heavenly abode,
There keep the life a hundred years.
Here thy protecting care extend,
There for a century guard the gift,
Here at the same time keep us from ills.

To *appease offended nats* is the sum total of Kachin religion. But this takes various forms according to different circumstances. If lightning strikes, the *nat* of thunder must have an offering or worse danger is at hand. If a house or a village burns, sacrifices must be made, and water sprinkled to send off the incendiary *nat,* (*Mauhte*), who is always abroad. If a man is drowned, killed by a falling tree, a tiger or an enemy, or if he loses his life in any kind of accident, the *nat* or genius causing such misfortunes must be placated or others will meet the same fate. If a woman dies in confinement the necessary ceremonies will be attended to, as otherwise the woman becomes a *nat* (*sawn*), whose special aim will be to bring others into the same trouble. In all such cases the object is to pacify the *nat,* that there may be no further mischief.

Protection and immunity from danger is closely related to this. But in this case it is prevention rather than cure that is sought. It is especially from the Fates and witches that evil is apprehended. If a man has been successful in a business venture, if he has prospered in his general work, if he becomes trusted and respected, people will surely discuss his merits or demerits and the "Fate of jealousy" will be aroused. Thus something is always offered to the "genius of aspersion" before and after a journey, business transaction, housebuilding, wedding, or the like. If a man knows he has enemies, it is necessary to guard against magic, curses and witches. In time of war sacrifices are offered to ascertain the will of the *nats,* to bless special charms, to determine lucky and unlucky days, and for general success. The offerings and ceremonies will vary according to the nature of the case. A fowl may be all that is needed to keep the Fates placable. But the "Fate of imprecation," appropriately demands a portion of wild ginger with the other offering. The dreaded "Fate of accidents" is propitiated by having a cinnamon tree riddled with bullets or studded with long bamboo spikes, indicating that thus they wish to deal with all unpleasant intruders, and a dog wound up in elephant grass is hung up in the next tree to keep the spirit from coming that particular road. If it is the cruel *Jăhtung* that holds a person prisoner, anything so small as an egg must not be considered. A dog, a goat or a sheep alone will satisfy him, and the preference nowadays is the dog. The head is cut off and the body is buried. To the *nat* causing insanity among the common people, (the *mădai* or *shădip* cause insanity among the chiefs, but the common people have nothing to do with these), similar offerings are made. When all other sacrifices have proved of no avail, a goat or a young buffalo is selected, and after appropriate ceremonies a part of the clothing of the afflicted party is tied to the horns and the animal is sent off into the dense jungle or lonely mountains. If the animal does not return, it is taken as a sign that the *nat* has departed and will give no further trouble. If it does return, it is allowed to roam about anywhere; no one lays claim to it, and no one would kill or eat the flesh as it is dedicated and belongs to the *nat* of insanity.

The desire for *riches and prosperity* is universal, and the gods or spirits have always been regarded as the dispensers of wealth and affluence. A rich harvest, a well filled barn, numerous pigs and fowls, skill and success in labor, a large family and a long life comprise the desires of the average Kachin. Gold and silver for the sake of hoarding is far above the wildest dreams of the ordinary man. Only the chiefs and some of the more enterprising among the elders accumulate silver (money), which they generally hide in some secret place near the house or in the jungle. Some believe that money not used in this life will be useful in the next, and thus never make known the hiding place. The following extract taken from the formula usually employed when riches and prosperity are solicited, will give a good idea of what is the burden of the prayer. (The original will be found in the Introduction to the Kachin Dictionary, page xxiii.)

Celestial chief and heavenly friend:
To women fullest wisdom send,
And men of knowledge ample store,
Grant red rice, white rice, grain of every kind.
Now with bovine riches is filled the house-front stable,
Crowded is the spacious barn, filled the granary.
An increase of a hundred cattle,
Multiplied a hundred head of cows.
Keep the old cow with curved horn,
Guard the old bull with dew-lap neck.
Coming are a hundred speckled cattle,
Added five score spotted cows.
With best fowls and breeding hogs,
Crowded are the spacious baskets,
Swarming under the great house floor.
Yes, hundred fowls, five score of pigs.
White rice, red rice, grain abounding,
Filled is the paddy-bin, packed the granary.
When eating old rice the new is added,
While using old yam the new is growing.
I teach mothers wisdom and children art,
And men the knowledge of town and mart;
To advocate, the priest and story-teller,
To soldier, blacksmith, the trader, seller,
I grant gold and riches, abounding wealth,
Abundant treasure, long life and health.
On wealth's high summit they now will stand
Enjoying happiness of gold and land.

Sowing and harvest festivals. The festivals and sacrifices connected with sowing and harvest are especially illustrative of the care taken to secure the goodwill of the guardians of home and village. When the jungle clearing for the year begins, a small offering may or may not be given. But just before the time of sowing a great festival, headed by the chief as representative of the whole community, is held at the village entrance (*măshang*), when the blessing of the earth-priest (*ga nat, shădip*), is sought. Only eggs, dried fish and whisky are offered in connection with the festival for the day; but towards evening in the presence of only the leading priests and the chief, a fowl or some dried fish is buried in the enclosure for the earth-*nat* (*shădip*). In some localities a cow or a pig is given and buried if by divination it is ascertained that such offerings are required, and the presence of the chief is not necessary. The priest having finished the ceremony, does not turn around, but reverently goes backward when he leaves. A four days holiday (*na na*) follows, during which time no work is done. At the close of the four days the diviner determines what particular household will have the privilege to begin the sowing. The chosen family makes a start and two more holidays follow. During this time offerings of eggs, fowls and liquor are in order. When the grain is about half grown there is another festive period of four days (*măyu na*), but less sacred than the first. There is another communal sacrifice headed by the chief, and offerings are presented according to the wishes of the *nats* as made known by divination. The long pole, hung with chicken baskets (*u yawm*) always seen at the beginning of the dry season at the village entrance, dates from this sacrifice. When the grain is ripening the "first fruit" is gathered and eaten by the family that made the first sowing. Then "new rice," the feast of the new rice (*nlung unan poi*), can be prepared and eaten by all. A part of the ceremony is that unripe rice (*ntsit*) is roasted (then called *mnyi*) and eaten by the family and friends. This is a time of general rejoicing and families come together in re-union. During the time of harvest and threshing a kind of thanksgiving is observed. The "spirit of the rice" is invoked and urged to remain in the granary, that there may be no loss, and that seed for the following year may be abundant. With the carrying home of the grain the last ceremony (*nhpang ba ai poi*) of the year takes place. A woman picks a few ears from a patch that has been left standing for the occasion, puts them in her basket and begins her homeward walk acting as though she was carrying a very heavy load. This to show that even small favors are appreciated. In connection with all these times and seasons the spirits are always remembered and appropriate offerings are made.

It will be seen that nearly all the regular holiday seasons are connected with the labor of the fields. When an accident has happened to an individual or a community; if a person has been killed by a tiger, by lightning, or drowned; if a house has burned or an epidemic has broken out, a holiday of one day only (*na tai*) is declared; all other seasons of rest comprise two or four days, an uneven number being unlucky. These days and seasons are as follows:

(1) Two days after the highland paddy-hut (*yi wa*) has been built by the whole community for the chief; usually the last part of March or early in April. This holiday is not observed in some localities.

(2) Two days when setting fire to the jungle clearing. There is a great deal of liberty allowed in regard to this observance.

(3) Four days just before sowing. This is the most solem occasion of the year and the great sacrifice of the chief (*nat sut*) takes place.

(4) Two days after the first family has started the sowing.

(5) Four days when the grain is growing (*măyu na*).

(6) Two days after the rice field belonging to the chief has been reaped by communal labor: this is, however, observed only in certain localities. Anything corresponding to a Sabbath, or days for especial religious observance connected with the changes of the moon, are unknown. In a few places in the Northern Shan States the bazaar day (coming every fifth day) is held as somewhat sacred, and paddy is not pounded in the morning of that day; but this is exceptional and is caused by a tradition that

it is unlucky to do this kind of work on the morning of that day.

The nats and disease. By far the greatest number of sacrifices are offered to secure help in time of illness. Almost everything afflicting a Kachin is attributed to the malevolence of the spirits. Disease, in spite of a healthy climate and a great deal of outdoor life, is very common, owing to the complete ignorance of hygenic and sanitary laws. The belief that the *nats* alone can help has developed a certain measure of fatalism in regard to health and bodily comfort. They often seem entirely indifferent to pain, but in reality they stand a great deal less than their civilized brothers. It is almost impossible to induce them to have a tooth pulled, however much it may ache; they will rather suffer than submit to a slight operation. As a rule they never seek medical aid until the case is too far gone and has become practically hopeless. He expects to the last a turn for the better, or else he simply looks upon it as his fate which it is useless to try to change. In case of a cold, four to eight days are allowed in which to take care of itself. If instead of improving the patient grows worse, it is taken for granted that the spirits are at work, and this is soon verified by divination. Incurable or chronic diseases are after some time given up, and the priest declares that this is a case of *ana,* (a malady), and that the *nats* have nothing to do with it. Goitre, for example, which is common all over the hills, is not attributed to the *nats,* but to salt introduced by the kalas (foreigners). Some kinds of boils, swellings and sores are caused by witches. In every case of ordinary trouble the spirits are consulted and the sacrifices and all the kinds of offerings mentioned amount to quite a sum throughout the year, even for a poor family. They will often go heavily in debt to satisfy the greed of their invisible tormentors. The Kachins often put it that they are "slaves to the *nats,*" and his slavery is both burdensome and exacting.

Ideas of a Supreme Being. While thus the everyday

religion of the Kachins is spirit worship, which originated in fear of the ancestral "shades," they have apparently always had an idea of a supreme power. A great spirit, *Kărai Kăsang,* is above all the *nats,* and he alone is the original Creator, he is the Supreme One. Several names are given to him, among them the Omniscient One. This being who knows all was especially manifested at the creation of man, and had then something like a human birth. There may be here some faint echo of an Indian incarnation myth, or we may deal with some transmigration story taken and reshaped from Buddhism. The Supreme One never had a human birth and how he came into existence no one can tell. Still the Creator (*Hpan wa Ningsan*), the Omniscient One (*Chye wa Ningchyan*), the One Higher than the Clouds, (*Sumwi Sumdam*), a term having almost a magical meaning with many, and the Supreme One (*N-gawn Kărai Kăsang*), are one and the same. It is true that a Kachin is hopelessly lost when attempting to explain how this one being could be born, and still be above everything that was born, and at the same time claim that he never had a mother. But we only need remember that more intelligent races have had similar difficulties in connection with their particular forms of theology. All a Kachin really claims to know is that there is someone higher and greater than the *nats.* Further than this we can know nothing about him. No altars are raised in his honor, no sacrifices are ever made to propitiate him, no one can know his abode or divine his will. He is immortal, omniscient, omnipotent and omnipresent, and this is never affirmed of the *nats.*

The knowledge of a supreme power exerts no particular moral influence over the Kachins. He is regarded as too far above man to take any interest in the everyday affairs of mortals. Only in extreme cases will he punish a hopelessly wicked individual, but when and how no one seems to know. But when a great calamity has befallen an individual or a community, when war, pestilence or

Sacrificial buffalo ready for slaughter.

P. 168.

famine is raging and the *nats* do not seem propitious or able to help, people will call in their distress to the Lord of all. But when the trouble has passed there is no further thought of him, and no form of worship exists by which homage or gratitude is shown.

In these thoughts, forms and ceremonies we see the relationship with the backward and illiterate races in all lands and ages. Spirit worship as evolved from fear and reverence for the departed is the religion nearest at hand to the savage. It is education and enlightenment that introduce higher forms of religious ideas.

We have left the religious ceremonies observed at birth, marriage and death to be considered in the following chapters. The Kachins make very little of the other world, and I am greatly surprised to read in Mr. Hodson's excellent account of "the Naga Tribes of Manipur," that among them the belief in a heaven seems to be quite prominent. The Nagas, Chins and Kachins are in most other particulars very nearly alike, and their religious ideas are almost identical. I must confess that I have my doubts as to the correctness of the interpretation of the faith of the Nagas in this particular. Equally surprising is it to find, that, "There is a selection according to the life lived in this world, where the 'good' so called go to one place and the 'bad' to another." This indicates a development in religious ideas far beyond the conception of the Kachins, and far beyond illiterate tribes in general. It may of course be that the Nagas have been influenced by Hinduism more than the Kachins ever have been by Buddhism.

CHAPTER XIV.

NATAL CEREMONIES.

The Kachins hail with delight every new addition to the family. A large number of children is an honor, as well as a sure sign of favor from the powers above. Besides, and probably the most important of all, it is a comfortable assurance of liberal support in old age. Every new arrival is looked upon as an additional bread-winner in time to come. The thought of how to support a large family never troubles the man of the house. He looks to the children to support him as soon as they can work; his responsibility ends when they are large enough to tend the cattle or pull weeds in the paddy-field.

Childbirth, like everything else, is hedged about with a great number of customs, rules and ceremonies. During pregnancy a woman must not eat honey or porcupine flesh, as these things will cause miscarriage. Yet there is very little let up in the work she has to do, and this with other causes already mentioned is the reason why miscarriages are rather common, and a large number of very weak children are born that die in their early years. Families without children are very numerous.

When a child is about to be born, the married women of the neighbourhood are called to assist in such matters as may be necessary, Midwives or medical assistance is unknown, and in difficult cases the mother generally succumbs. As soon as the sex of the babe is known one of the attendant women pronounces its name. This is done in order to prevent ill disposed *nats* from naming the child first, as in such a case it will sicken and die.

Cutting the navel. After naming the child comes the navel-cutting ceremony. A sharp splint of bamboo is cut from a post in the wall and is used as a knife. As an odd number is unlucky, two or four such splints are cut, but only one is used. The "knife" being ready the knee of the babe is brought up to the abdomen and the navel is cut the length of the knee. The navel and the placenta are usually buried by the middle post at the side of the steps at the front door. It is incased in thirty pair of bamboo splits wound and tied by twenty pair of splits (*păli*) used for tying purposes. A fence of thorns is made around the place so as to keep animals away, and two spears are put up, remaining four days in the case of a male, and three in the case of a female.

Natal feasts. If everything is successful a "small" meal (*chyăyen*) is eaten by the old people. Dried meat, dried fish and ginger are the only dishes at this time. Children must not partake of this meal, as they, if they do so, will grow up with a jealous disposition. After this there is the regular feast (*jăhtaw*) of which all are allowed to partake. Here too the principal dishes are rice, dried meat and ginger. In eating, and of course drinking, to the health and long life of the child, the following blessing is pronounced by a priest or some elderly person:

> This morning's natal food is pleasant and palatable;
> May you live till your hair is gray,
> May you live till your teeth have fallen off,
> Till you can do nothing but sit and frighten the hawks,
> Till the dust of the front stable covers your body.

Friends and relatives now congratulate the happy parents and bring the usual gifts. Those particularly interested present the same kind of spear and sword as are given at a wedding.

Presenting the child to the nats and to the sun. The mother and child must remain in the house until the fourth day in the case of a male, and until the third if it is a female. As it is always unlucky to end up anything on an odd day, the fourth day in the case of a girl, is her wedding day, when she has a "second birth," becomes a "woman" and remains in the house of her husband. On the fourth or the third day the village priests, neighbours and friends gather for the ceremony of presenting the new born child to the family *nats*. A priest places some dried fish and meat, a dried mole or rat, some liquor and malted rice before the household *nats*, asking their favor and protection in behalf of the new member of the family. Having presented the child to the supernatural guardians, an old man or woman takes the new arrival for the presentation to the sun. Starting from the place opposite the family altar, the child is carried past the chief fire-place and then taken back again, while the words: "Go out and see the sun, come and behold the sun," are repeated both in going and returning. Having made this turn inside the house, the child is now carried to the threshhold of the front door, and back again to the back door, the same words being pronounced in each case. The child can now be carried outdoors by anyone.

The purification of the mother. On the day when the child is presented to the family *nats* the mother performs her purification and again takes her place in the community. The husband, or some delegated male member of the family, takes a spear, and the woman her soiled garments, and both proceed to the village spring, where the woman in silence washes herself and the clothing. Returning, the woman goes first and the man follows. This is done to keep off any unfriendly *nats* that may be contemplating mischief to the mother and child.

Death in confinement, (*ndang kăpaw*). Death in confinement is one of the greatest and most dreaded calamities that can befall a family, and the greatest curse that can be pronounced upon a woman is that she will meet such an end. When parturition is attended with special difficulties, and by divination it is ascertained that an evil spirit, called *sawn* or *ndang*, is trying to prevent the birth of the child, the wildest and most distressing excitement takes place. Crowds gather around the house; every road and path is blockaded; guns are fired, arrows and mud-pellets are shot in every direction around and under the house; swords and torches are brandished over the woman; some-one in possession of a charm, especially a thunder-bolt, places it on the back of her head; all kinds of impossible means are tried to assist her; red-pepper, bark of several kinds, old rags, or in fact anything that will produce a pungent, noisome smell, is burned to drive away the dreaded intruder, and to prevent "her" (the *nat*) from carrying away the woman and child. But these things generally prove of no avail and the unfortunate woman dies for want of more practical assistance. She has now herself become a *sawn*, and as she will long for company she will try to bring other women into the same difficulty. Consequently she is at once cremated. If the child died with the mother they are burned together. If the child is living it is placed by the side of the mother. If it cries when with the corpse, and quiets down when taken away, it is a sign that it does not wish to "go with" the mother. If, however, it cries when away from the dead body and remains quiet when with the corpse, it is interpreted to mean that the child will not be separated from the mother, and it is thus burned on the same funeral pyre. Apart from this, infanticide is unknown among the hill tribes.

Names. The names of the first seven males in every Kachin family are those borne by the seven primitive *nats*, and the seven ruling sons of the great ancestor *Wahkyet wa*. They always come in the same order, and indicate that the child is the first, second, third, etc., among the males. These names in their order are as follows: *Gam, Naw, La, Tu, Tang, Yaw* and *Hka*. During childhood a boy is as a rule called *Ma Gam, Ma Naw, Ma La*, etc., *Ma* being the word for child. When grown he becomes *N-Gam, N-Naw, N-La* and so on, and if of some especial importance he is addressed as *La N-Gam, La N-Naw, La N-La*, etc., the word *La* emphasizing the fact that he is a man. The male members of a chief's family carry the title *Zau* (*jau*), a term borrowed from the Shan, meaning Lord. Thus we have *Zau Gam, Zau Naw, Zau La, Zau Tu*, etc., (Compare Appendix II.)

As it would be impossible to distinguish between all the *Ma Gam's, Ma Naw's*, etc., in the same village, a boy is either provided with a nick-name (*mying-hkawt*), which is usually a term of endearment or indicative of his place and position, or else the family name is given before his real name. Thus a *Ma Gam* may be called *Ma Shawng* to indicate that he is the first born, *Lăbya Gam*, showing that he comes from the *Lăbya* family, or *Zau Gam*, indicating that he is the first son of a chief. A *Ma Naw* may in the same way be called *Ma Grawng* or *Naw Grawng*, the "addition," *Nhkum Naw* or *Zau Naw*. As the family names are very numerous, the difficulty of distinguishing between the limited number of personal names is not as great as it would at first appear. Only a few of these nick-names need to be given. They are in reality endless and vary in different localities:

A *Zau Gam* may be called: *Zau Ri, Sengli, Hkun Seng, Jali*, etc.

A *Ma Gam* may be called: *Ma Shawng, Ma Brang, Shawng Brang, Kam Htoi, Shawng wa*, etc.

A *Ma Naw* may be called: *Baw Naw, Grawng Naw, Ning Grawng*, etc.

A *Ma La*, may be called: *La Nau, La Doi*, etc.

A *Ma Tu*, may be called: *Lum, Tu Lum*, etc.

A *Ma Tung*, may be called: *Gun, Ma Gun*, etc.

A *Ma Yaw*, may be called: *Htung, Yaw Htung*, etc.

A *Ma Hka*, may be called: *Tawm, Hka Tawm*, etc.

Female names follow the same category. The first seven girls in a family are called in the order as they are born, *Kaw, Lu, Roi, Htu, Kai, Hka* and *Pri*. The word *Ma* is usually prefixed and thus we have *Ma Kaw, Ma Lu, Ma Roi*, etc. The daughters of a chief carry the title *Nang*, also a Shan term. Names of endearment or distinguishing terms, as in the case of the boys, are also given to the girls, but they are as a rule not called by the family name. Some of the names for girls are the following:

A *Nang Kaw* becomes *Nang Seng, Nang Mun, Nang Shawng,* etc.

A *Ma Kaw* becomes *Ma Shawng, Hkin Nan, Chyem, Kaw Lum,* etc.

A *Ma Lu* becomes *Baw, Ma Baw, Baw Tawng, Nem,* etc.

A *Ma Roi* becomes *Ji, Roi Ji, Nau, Roi Nau,* etc.

A *Ma Htu* becomes *Ma Lum, Htu Lum,* etc.

A *Ma Kai* becomes *Htang, Ma Htang,* etc.

A *Ma Hka* becomes *Tawm, Hka Tawm,* etc.

A *Ma Pri* becomes *Pri Lum, Ma Ti,* etc.

Names for an additional nine boys and eight girls are provided in case a family should be thus singularly blessed. There are,

MALES:	FEMALES:
Shăroi,	*N-Yun,*
N-Yun,	*N-Kying,*
N-Kying.	*Kying Nang,*
Kying Nang,	*Kying Htang,*
Kying Htang,	*Ka Htang,*
Ka Htang,	*Ka Rang,*
Ka Rang,	*Tsup Ni,*
Tsup Ni,	*Tsup Nawn.*
Tsup Nawn.	

The inventive skill in nomenclature having failed after the first eight of each kind, the names for boys and girls become the same.

General remarks. Probably there is more diversity in regard to customs and usages connected with childbirth, than in regard to any other particular of the family or communal life. Each group of families is sure to have some peculiarities all its own, observed at this important occasion. In regard to women who have died at childbirth there are various beliefs and consequent ceremonies in

Altars in front of house.

Cremation.

P. 176.

different sections of the country. In the Gauri hills, for instance, and also in certain other localities, the belief is that the "spirits" (*sawn* or *ndang num ni,* the "women" who cause the obstruction), who are responsible for this sad misfortune, are not afraid of guns, and thus no guns are fired. They fear only bows for shooting mud pellets (*lăhpaw*), as with those it is possible to hit their eyes. In addition to the means just mentioned, there are in some localities a disgusting display of the male private parts, for the sake of driving away (*je kau ai*) these troublesome and invisible females.

Also in the ceremonies of cutting the navel there is some diversity. Some mothers give the little one some chewed rice almost immediately after it is born, but it does not seem to be a general custom. In the main the customs outlined are those that have the preference.

CHAPTER XV.

MARRIAGE CEREMONIES.

Courtship as known in civilized lands is unknown among the Kachins. A "love-match" is next to impossible, because of the family customs which consider marriage a question of economy, to be considered and settled like any other bargain. Young people, living in the same community may and do take a liking to each other, although it is certain they never "fall in love" as we understand the expression, and on account of the great freedom granted before marriage, it often results in promiscuous intercourse, and the girl becomes the "mother of a bastard," (*n-gyi kănu*). But it is seldom marriage follows such relations. There is always a certain amount of disgrace attached to marrying a "bastard-mother," and besides it may not be agreeable to the parents of either party. The young man and his family prefer to settle matters by the paying of a fine to the damsel's parents, (See Chap. VI), and then both are free to find companions in the regular way as recognized by custom.

The Kachins are thoroughly oriental in their marriage relations. The parents of the contracting parties settle all the details and the young people have nothing to say about it. A particularly strong-minded girl, if she finds the man selected for her especially objectionable, may defy the parental wishes, but such cases are rare. They are becoming more and more common under modern conditions, for reasons we will mention later on. The girl is regarded as the "salable" property of her parents, and being bought with a "price," becomes the inseperable property of her husband's family. A Kachin man never says "I have taken a wife;" his family always put it, "We have married a woman," meaning that they have paid the price for her and she belongs to them. If her husband dies, she goes by right to the next younger brother, or else becomes the servant of the household, unless it is agreed to give her to some near relative. Polygamy is permitted, but not at all common. It costs too much to procure a new wife, and very few can afford to pay for more than one. Most men who have more than one wife have come into possession by "picking up widows" (*gaida hta*) left by brothers or near relatives.

Consanguinity. Marriage is allowed only between certain recognized families; but the old rules are more and more disregarded and greater liberties are allowed. According to strict ancestral custom persons having the same family name can never intermarry. A *Lăhpai* chief, for example, could never marry the daughter of another *Lăhpai* chief, even though there were no blood relation between them from our point of view. A *Lăbya* man can never take a *Lăbya* women; to do so would be "incest" (*jaiwawng*), as they have the same surname. This rule did not inconvenience commoners particularly, as there are any amount of families to choose from, but it did work hardship within the families of the chiefs, as their wife procuring sphere was limited to the five ruling families. These bonds have been broken through and intermarriage is now practiced between the recognized divisions of the same family. Thus a *Gauri Lăhpai* can marry a woman of the *Hpunggan Lăhpai.* An *Nhkum* from one branch of the family may marry into another branch of the same name, provided it is certain that there is no actual blood relation between them. The families of chieftains take greater liberties along these lines than commoners. Among the latter the ancestral practice is still followed rather closely. A chief can marry a commoner, but it seldom happens. He must as a rule find the daughter of a chief. A commoner cannot marry the daughter of a chief,—but nowadays it does happen where education and modern conditions make the old landmarks impossible. All relationship is reckoned from the male side; the woman's identity is lost the moment she unites with her husband and his family. As a rule both a chief and a commoner aim to marry a first cousin, the daughter of the mother's brother. There is from a Kachin point of view no relationship between these children. The mother has come from a family with a different name, and her brothers cannot marry into the family she has become identified with, but must go in a different direction; thus there are no family relations (*măyu dama*) in the way, they are only incidentally (*tăwu lăhta*) connected. But it is not compulsory, and no customs are violated if a wife is sought somewhere else. It is useless even to attempt to say what families can intermarry nowadays. We know what was generally the custom twenty or twenty-five years ago. Then among the chiefs it was customary that,

A *Mărip* chief married the daughter of a *Măran* chief,

A *Măran* sought his bride among the *N-Hkums,*

A *N-Hkum,* went to a branch of the *Lăhpai* family, (*Gauri Atsi, Hpunggan*).

A *Lăhpai* would seek a spouse among the *Lăhtaws* or *Mărans.*

A *Lăhtaw* would be accommodated by the *Mărips* or *Lăhpais.*

While in a general way these customs are still observed, there is, as we have already said, a tendency to override these narrow restrictions. Among commoners, for a man to marry a woman with the same surname is looked upon as irregular, but it is done and will be done more and more. Consanguinity is, however, strictly forbidden,—

(1) With a father's sister's child, as the blood of her fathers (that of her brothers), is still in her veins even though by law she bears a different name.

(2) A paternal uncle's children, as they are "brothers and sisters" having the same surname. There is no word for cousin on the paternal side, all are ***hpu nau,*** brothers and sisters; a father's sister's children are also

brothers and sisters, but all children of the mother's sisters are cousins (***hkau*** or ***hkri***).

(3) A mother's sister's child, as they are cousins, and may be "brothers and sisters," as she may marry in the same family as the mother.

These restrictions are not violated; it would be a great disgrace to disregard them. Marriages of sisters and half-sisters has apparently never been practiced, and the generally prohibited degrees of intermarriage are observed. In these things our Kachins are as strict and particular as any civilized people can be.

Abduction. There are two ways of procuring a wife: abduction, and a formal proposal. The former method is resorted to if the maiden's family are unreasonable and ask too much for their daughter. In that case the man's family send some emissaries to the girl's village, who there secure the assistance of an "elder" and some of the young people. The girl in question is led by a decoy to the village of the young man. There she is forced through the religious ceremony and is bound for life. But if the parents follow and arrive before she has passed the sacred elephant grass they can prevent the marriage. As a rule, however, the matter is settled in a peaceful way. The elder, who is in the secret, goes to the parents the morning after the girl has left, he shows them the presents, and as they are on the recognized scale, even if not all they originally asked, they find it best to acquiesce. This way of getting a wife "cheap," is still in practice, although it is far from the general proceedings. Under British rule there is still a cheaper way which is becoming more and more popular. Young people with something of modern ideas will marry because they like each other, and if the parents object they can run away and settle down in some community away from home. These innovations are greatly deplored by the old conservatives, who think young people are not what they used to be, and that the times are getting out of joint. Still, neither abduction nor elopement are the rule. By far the greatest number of marriages take place according to the ancestral customs, and our concern is now with the rules and regulations necessary for a strictly Kachin nuptial.

The preliminaries. When the parents of a young man think it is time for him to have a wife, or rather when they desire a daughter-in-law to work for them, they procure some small articles from all the likely girls of families with which intermarriage is permissable and customary. A diviner is sent for, and the articles, some yarn, chewing lime, a coonbot, a piece of cloth, an article of dress or anything belonging to the girl, are tested by divination. The diviner places the articles representing the different maidens separately and in line, and touching each object in turn with the "divining bamboo," he by his art determines which one will prove the best wife, and bring the most happiness and prosperity. As a rule there must be several tests before a satisfactory reply is obtained, and the next step in taken.

The proposal. When the divination has given the desired information, and it is made clear that a certain maiden is destined to become the wife of the young man in question, an experienced emissary is sent to negotiate matters with the prospective parents-in-law (*măyu ni*). He and his companions proceed to the village and engage the services of some leading man (*sălang*, elder) of that community. This elder proceeds to the home of the intended and opens up negotiations with her family. The elder prepares himself with half a bottle of liquor brought by the real go-between, and the other half goes to the father of the maiden. He urges his case with skill, reminding the parents that the family seeking their daughter is well to do and respectable; that the girl is of marriageable age; that it is wise to find her a husband before she goes wrong and becomes a disgrace to her parents. The girl's family now ask for the pedigree of the young man, and particulars as to the standing and prosperity of his parents. They particularly wish to know if they are of respected lineage, and if there have ever been any witches among them. If all is satisfactory, the liquor is accepted and the reply is given, "Well, it is as you wish." In most cases, however, so important an affair demands several visits from the delegate, a great deal of consultation is necessary, and the girl's family, with an eye to business, try to drive as close a bargain as possible. But there is no law forbidding the matter being settled the first time; it is all "as it happens."

If the elder has been successful, he returns to his house where the emissaries have been waiting. These have now in readiness the "evening presents," (*nsin ja*), so called because these affairs are always discussed around the evening fire. The presents as a rule consist of a dried squirrel or a mole wrapped up in two blankets, some silk or woolen cloth. Of course such presents vary, and there are in most localities different standards for chiefs and commoners. Our concern throughout is with the regulations observed by the chiefs. The line of procedure is the same in each case, but presents and the price paid are on a larger scale (more than double), when a chief is married. When the evening presents have been accepted, the date of the marriage and other particulars can be discussed.

The emissaries from the man's family are notified that so far all has progressed satisfactorily, and they now enter the house of the prospective bride, and the real bargaining begins. The elder first called by the emissaries represents the "asking family" (*dama ni*), and a second elder attends to the interests of the "giving family" (*snăyu ni*). The question, how much to pay for the girl is the all absorbing subject. The first elder, in the interest of his clients, and incidentally of his own, tries to procure the damsel as cheaply as possible, while the second elder, with similar motives, argues for a liberal allowance. This part of the programme is probably never settled in one evening and it may take weeks and even months before there is a final agreement. The price for the daughter of a chief in the good old times use to be: one bullock, called the "liquor carrying bullock;" rupees one hundred "viss of silver;" one slave (*shingma lai-măyam*), to carry on the work formerly done by the girl; one roll of Chinese embroidery; some felt cloth; a rhinoceros horn and an elephant tusk; a long, richly embroidered Chinese coat; an old gong; a large far-sounding gong ten spans in circumference; ten cows; one buffalo to be sacrificed and eaten by the subjects of the chief on the wedding day; a string of valuable beads, especially intended to open the "hand and heart" of the mother, that she may be willing to part with her daughter. This represents quite a good deal of property even for a chief, and few can nowadays pay the price. Slaves, elephant tusks and rhinoceros horns are no longer in the market, and cattle or money must be substituted. The poverty of the present times makes it impossible to attain to the ancestral glory. The full price is seldom, if ever, paid before the marriage, and it may take years and years before the last cow or rupee has found its way to the giving family, who never forget to remind their sons-in-law of the amount still lacking.

For a commoner the price is more moderate, but still heavy enough. It includes cattle, (slaves in well-to-do families), felt-cloth, a gong or two, a blanket, a silk-jacket, rupees ten, and anything else that can be extorted. It will readily be seen how neither commoner nor chief could afford to keep a large harem with such prices for women. If the wife ever complains that she has to work too hard, the husband always reminds her of the heavy price he had to pay, and he regards it as his right to get his money back.

Leaving the parental home. When the day for the wedding (*kumba shălai*), has arrived, the maiden leaves the parental home. Father, mother or near relatives never attend the wedding, which is always held at the bridegroom's house. The girl is at this occasion seen without the baskets always carried by the women. It is the only time she ever appears on the road without a burden on her back. She is attended by a certain number of followers, namely: one elder and an elderly woman delegated by her family; one bridesmaid carrying a large basket of gifts (*kumba lit*) from the parents, and another with a smaller basket; the elder acting as the first negotiator, and a man appointed to kill the wedding pig. This is the official list, but in addition as many as wish may follow, and there is usually a big gathering. Two spears and two swords are found in each of the baskets carried by bridesmaids; besides they contain samples of grain and vegetables of all kinds valued by the Kachin. These baskets signify that the bride is bringing prosperity to her new home. The followers in addition carry one spear with which to dig the hole for the sacred elephant grass, and one sword with which to notch the log, used as a new stairway, by which the bride enters the new home. The man appointed to kill the pig carries his own sword.

Before leaving the home the younger sister presents her with such silver ornaments as are in fashion. If she has elder sisters she must appease them with gifts for the privilege of marrying before them. The parents give her as a dowry a slave and a pony; poor people give whatever they can afford. The buffalo given for the purpose is killed and the village people have a feast. If the family is wealthy and generous one may be killed the day after. As a parting gift the emissaries present the beads to the bride's mother. The party moves to the house of the elder (*janghtung*), and from there the procession takes its way to the bridegroom's village where they stay in the house of the emissaries (*kăsa ni a nta*), until everything is ready for the marriage ceremony.

The ceremony. Before the arrival of the emissaries and the bride, some individual is sent, (probably two or three days before), to announce that an agreement has been reached, and that the woman will be on her way. Everything is then arranged, and friends and relatives are called. The sacrifices are set apart, the elephant grass to be used is cut, the house is set in order and an abundance of food and drink is provided. On the morning of the great day all the village people gather at the house and try to make themselves generally useful. Some cut and square a fresh log, which after being notched, is used as a ladder or stairway for the "new woman" (*num ningnam*), to step on when she enters her future home; others spread the mats and cut blocks of wood to serve as stools for the bride and the principle guests. The arrangement of the elephant grass is an important part of the ceremony. There is a hole dug for each of the family *nats* represented, and for each of the "Fates" (*măraw*). The holes are dug in a straight line with the front gable of the house. The household *nats* take the side nearest the house, the "Fates" take the end away from the dwelling place. The bundles of elephant grass are dropped into holes dug with the spear brought for the occasion, but the holes are not filled in. When the grass has been placed, a squared log about six feet long is placed so as to divide the grass representing the household *nats* into two equal parts, but the grass in honor of the Fates is all turned to one side. There are as a rule three bunches of grass representing the household *nats*, and three in honor of the Fates. The "three Fates" on this occasion are of the bridegroom's house, the bride's family, and of the emissaries. Each bunch of grass also represents an offering to the respective *nat* in question. To the household divinities cattle and pigs are presented, the Fates are satisfied with fowls. A different priest must officiate at each of the offerings, and he takes some of the grass from the bunch representing the *nat* he is serving, and waves it before him as he officiates. This part of the ceremony usually takes a good part of a forenoon, and the people come together for the main event.

While these offerings are presented, the bride, who has remained in the house of the go-between, is led forth by the delegated old people, while the young men and women go out to meet her, pounding gongs and drums, singing and even dancing. (The dancing is by some young man particularly skilled in the art.) The damsel is placed on a new stool on a large bamboo mat; her followers and representatives of her family are also honored with new stools on felt mats. Her future husband is now presented to her; it is most likely the first time they ever met. The bride's family through their representatives now have the last chance to enrich themselves on account of their daughter. If there is anything they have not asked for during the long days of negotiations, they now do it, enforcing their demands with the threat that if their request is not granted, the girl will not move a step further and there will be no wedding. There may be hours of pleading and arguing, or it may take only a few minutes to come to an understanding, but as a rule the bride's family have their way and the most important part of the act takes place.

When the last word in regard to the price has been spoken, and everything else is ready, two old man carrying bamboo vessels filled with liquor approach the priest representing the woman's family, and ask permission to kill the sacrificial hog. The priest steps forth and with a sacred sword, (a big, black, unsharpened iron sword never used except ceremonially), draws a line across the neck of the hog and then decapitates it with his regular sword. The blood is sprinkled on the two rows of elephant grass and on the log between. The bride now steps forth led by one or two female relatives, steps on the post and passes between the grass, followed by the bridesmaids and some distant relatives. Those not related to her pass by on either side, and all move towards the house of the bridegroom. In some localities a priest follows the bride, touching her forehead with a loop of elephant grass, signifying that anything improper and unlucky must be left behind. Reaching the stairway the bride steps on the new steps and at the front door stands the mother-in-law who welcomes her new daughter, and places a string of beads around her neck. She is then conducted to the mother-in-law's fire-place and all her new relatives are introduced. Her bridesmaids follow her, but the young men in the party stay behind in the place where the young people are allowed to meet.

Now begins the more festive part of the occasion. The representatives of the bride's family when entering the house, modestly settle down at the lower fire-place where the young people gather. The chief of ceremonies, now representing the bridegroom's family, begs them to step up to the chief fire-place and sit in the place of honor. They accept the invitation and as a token of appreciation place a spear at the corner of the fire-place. They are presented with eggs and cotton-cloth and they must be the first to partake of the wedding feast. They are liberally supplied with food and drink, and they praise the generosity of the house. Then betel nut, lime, tobacco, tea and other things used in friendly exchange of courtesy are presented, and the village people and others interested present gifts, mostly of liquor and vegetables, and become acquainted with the new woman.

Blessing the bride. On the evening of the wedding day there is a test to find out if the bride has a "straight" or "crooked" mind. A large boiler filled with rice-gruel is placed before her. If she can take the boiler and in one attempt place it straight on the tripod over the fire, her mind is "straight." As Kachin women are skilled in these particulars, it is seldom a failure is recorded. There is general rejoicing; small pieces of the skin from the animals sacrificed are put in with the gruel, and it is served to all around in plantain leaves.

If there is a village bard procurable he is likely to be called and will sing the ancestral story of the bride and bless her future career. The two spears carried by the bridesmaids are now brought forth; to each is tied securely two divining bamboos and ears of a kind of millet.

These "spears of blessing," as they are called, represent the father and the mother of the bride and are placed by the fire-place of the bridegroom's parents: between them is placed a server containing food made up of glutenous rice, eggs and boiled meat. The *Jaiwa* (high-priest), of the community, after having liberally imbibed of the freely flowing liquor, now begins his recital which will last all night long. As it is now late in the evening all are more or less under the influence of drink, but as a rule the crowd is orderly. The *Jaiwa* will recite a couplet from his long story and those particularly interested, and especially novices in training, will repeat it after him. In this way he will rehearse in rhythmic language the story of the first bridal pair, and the particular history of the bride, ending with wishing her a large number of children, and a long, happy and prosperous life. When a chief is married the wish is expressed that they may increase and multiply like the fruit of the sacred fig-tree. In the case of a commoner a less expressive illustration is used. The "food of blessing" placed between the "spears of blessing" is eaten together with a certain kind of rice-hash the next morning, and is then called "public food" (*tam ya shat*). A "roll" of the hash (or rice) is placed in the bridegroom's hand, who puts it up to the mouth of the bride, and she eats a little of it; the bride returns the compliment and this is the first meal of the happy couple. After the bridal pair have tasted the *tam ya shat*, all can partake of this food, which is sure to bring blessings especially to those who may at that time be matrimonially inclined.

The return of the bridal party. The main ceremony is over, the guests have scattered, but it still remains to get rid of the insatiable representatives of the bride's family, who like leeches hang on to the last. Baskets are woven and meat from the offerings with rice, liquor, cloth and gongs, are made up into two loads for the consolation of the lonely parents. They again through their representatives present another spear acknowledging their acceptance and satisfaction. The bridesmaids and other followers must not be forgotten and their remuneration may be about the following: the elder that escorted the bride, some silk-cloth; the woman on the same mission, about five rupees worth of stuff; the largest of the two maids, about rupees five, the smaller one rupees three; the elder who did the bargaining, one cow; the man who killed the pig, some woolen cloth or money. The other followers are given according to means and pleasure anything from a felt mat to some betel nut and tobacco. Having obtained their presents they are carried past the village entrance where the parting word is spoken, and then they start for home. If they have to be several days on the road, they can use the provision sent for the bride's family, but if it is only a day's journey they must deliver everything intact. With this their mission in ended.

After the wedding is over the bride remains inside her new home four days, spending most of her time preparing malted rice. On the fourth day the special friends of the family have a small wind up of the ceremonies, and eat and drink whatever is left. The bride is entitled to make three visits, (usually styled that she runs away three times), to her parental home, and the bridegroom and his family are never sure that she will return to them again. The first (*lanen nhtang*), about six or eight days after the marriage is to show her affection for her parents and home; the second (*kumba nhtang*), which takes place before the elephant grass is removed, is an ordinary, friendly visit; and the third, founded on an old tradition (*taugu hkăbang la nhtang*), has in view the bringing of the last of the bride's belongings to her new home. If the bride's parents are not satisfied with the gifts received, they have a right to keep her at home after one of these visits, on the condition that they return what already has been paid. But if they are satisfied, they will send back their daughter to her new home, and after the third time she is forever settled in her new surroundings. Cases are however not uncommon when after these visits she actually runs away and remains in her own home. If the parents cannot prevail on her to return, and she takes up relations with former lovers, there may be a feud and a debt (*hka*) to pay; but it is not a case for divorce, as it is not regarded as adultery. A small fine, or simply a promise that it will not happen again may be sufficient to square matters. Adultery (infidelity in the case of a wife who may have had children), was nearly always punished with death. But as a rule the Kachin marriage relations, though not ideal, are as happy as we have a right to expect. Wife-beating is rather the exception. The wife has a great deal of influence in the home and as she grows older she becomes honored and respected, especially if she is the proud mother of a large number of boys.

Marriage between Kachins and other races, Shans, Burmans and Chinese is not unknown, but not at all common. In days gone by wealthy chiefs would have one or more Shan wives, and now and then a Burman woman. In all such cases the children were treated as Kachins and some of the more intelligent families show unmistakeable traces of this mixed parentage. Weddings of this kind were nearly always conducted in accordance with the customs and usages of the woman's people.

Men making burial decorations.

Village burial march.

P. 192.

CHAPTER XVI.

FUNERAL CEREMONIES.

All Kachins believe in a life after this; but this faith has no practical importance or bearing in regard to conduct or morals in the present life. There is no attempt to prepare for the hereafter by any special rules or ceremonies. Hence their belief in the life to come can hardly be called a part of their religion; it is simply the inevitable that all must face; it is accepted as a part of the order of things. Death is not feared by the savage nearly as much as by the civilized man. A Kachin does not wish to talk about death; but when the hour comes, the individual and those around him await the final struggle with stoical calmness and indifference. The crying and lamentation, (generally by a few old women or the nearest female relatives), is a part of the program in connection with the obsequies. No doubt in many cases there is genuine grief, but the mourners are soon resigned and composed, accepting the inevitable. In regard to the future the belief is simply this: there is a life after this, lived in the ancestral realms, where conditions are about the same as upon earth. Further than this a Kachin, left to himself, has never advanced.

The spirit (*tsu*). Every individual at the moment of death becomes a spirit (*tsu*), which is different from the ghost (*minla*). The ghost is a kind of an astral body while the spirit is looked upon as a half-*nat* bound for the ancestral regions. This place, the abode of all disembodied spirits unless they return to their former habitations, is designated by different terms of which the most common are, *Tsu ga,* the land of the shades or spirits; *Kătsan ga,* the far away country; *Jat na ga,* the land of the perpetual increase, the abode of the departed, and *Jiwoi ga,* the ancestral realms. The spirit must pass the *Nhpraw hka,* (the white river) where it washes off all the defilement of earth, and putting on the forehead and appearance of a monkey, proceed to the cross-road that leads to the ancestral abodes. There are no very definite ideas as to the nature of the life in this mysterious realm; but the general impression is that the life on the other side is much like the present. The spirits have a kind of a body and stand in need of food (the evening haze); they can make use of slaves, weapons, money and agricultural implements. But as to all this there is a great diversity of opinion, and the funeral customs throw very little light on the subject. Funeral ceremonies follow the ancestral customs without any attempt to explain the why and wherefore. The present day Kachin may know nothing about the original meaning attached to the rites and ceremonies he follows. He repeats them because it is the custom and there he leaves it. This is not an uncommon experience in higher walks of civilization.

Influenced by Buddhism. While the reality of a life after this is accepted as an undisputed fact, there is no conception of an endless existence or immortality. That the departed pass over into the ancestral realms and there remain is a settled conviction; but whether they are alive, say a thousand years from now, and if so, in what condition they find themselves, are questions that have never troubled them, or claimed their attention. They would affirm or deny nothing as to the possibilities of the hereafter. In some localities where Shan influence is in evidence, there is a belief in *Mong Liban,* the *Nigban* or *Nirvana* of Buddhism. To this place the good and the worthy are admitted. But while they have borrowed the names from Buddhism, the conception of the place comes nearer the Christian idea of heaven than the traditional idea of *Nigban.* Annihilation or cessation of existence are propositions as far above their range of thinking, as the ideas of immortality or an endless eternity. There is a widespread faith in the possibility of transmigration, but few claim a personal belief along this line, and still fewer hold that they have lived in former ages. In the Northern Shan States we here and there meet old Kachins who claim to remember their past stages of existence, but these are exceptions, and they have left the true Kachin faith behind. Naturally where there is a tendency to belief in the Buddhist heaven, and the idea of transmigration is regarded as a possibility, the faith in a hell would not be absent. The knowledge of the Shan *Mong Ngărai di,* the cauldron of hell (Burma *ngăye*), conveys to the average Kachin an idea of a place of punishment and torment. But there is no particular fear of the place, and these ideas introduced from the outside have never been incorporated into their real faith and life. In the ancestral traditions, as rehearsed at every funeral, there is no mention of either *Mong Ngărai di,* (or as some say *Mong Hpyi ga,* the *nat* country), or *Mong Liban.* The spirit proceeds directly from this life to the land of the hereafter; there is only one way to follow, and only one place allotted for the descendants of *Chyănun* and *Wahkyet wa.*

Inhumation. Persons having died by accident (*lasa si,*) by drowning, killed by tigers, struck by lightning, etc., and women who have died in confinement, are cremated. If buried in the usual way they would become malignant *nats* who would lead others into the same kinds of misfortune that ended their lives. Insane persons are buried standing with an earthen pot covering the head. All others are interred with elaborate and expensive funeral ceremonies. There is with the Kachins, as with so many other primitive races, a desire for ostentatious obsequies, especially if it is an old man or woman who is conducted on the last journey. Children belive that they especially honor the parents if they give them a burial according to the best they can afford, and the departed will bless them accordingly.

Order of funeral ceremonies. The obsequies consist of two distinct parts. There are, first, the burial (*lup măkoi* or *mang hta kau ai*), which merely disposes of the corpse, (*mang*), while the spirit (*tsu*), remains in the old home, inhabiting the *nat*-place. The next and much more important step is the hiding of the corpse (*mang măkoi*), by which is meant the sending away of the spirit to the ancestral realms. The second act may take place weeks, months or even years after the interment of the corpse. The final honors to the departed is a most expensive affair, especially if it is a chief, or old and prominent people. A general idea of the different parts of the ceremony will be gained by having in mind the number of sacrifices from the day of the demise to the moment the spirit is conducted on the road to the land of the ancestral shades. There are two kinds of offerings, the first of which are absolutely necessary, the second class are more or less voluntary. The necessary offerings are the communal sacrifices (*măyawng shingkyawng hkungga*), of which mourners and all partake; the voluntary gifts (*jahpu shărut hkungga*), are especially intended for the spirit, and only old people can join in the sacrificial meal. Anyone is at liberty to add as many offerings and sacrifices to the regular number as inclination and ability dictate. The necessary offerings, which also indicate the steps followed in the funeral ceremonies, are the following:

When shrouding, washing and removing the corpse (*mang shăkru ai*), one bullock and one fowl.

When placed in state (*mang jang*), one fowl.

When making the coffin (*dău daw*), one fowl.

When putting up the *kăroi* (*kăroi jaing*), one cow or a buffalo.

When dancing in front of the house (*ndaw kăhkrang*), one fowl.

When digging the grave (*lup* or *nsung hku htu*), one fowl.

When starting the death-dance (*kăbung dum shawn*), one fowl.

When putting the spirit to sleep (*tsu shăyup ai*), one hog.

When arousing the spirit (*tsu jăs*), one hog.

When gathering wood for the funeral ceremonies (*hpun hta*), one hog.

When making general preparations (*lăhpaw htat*, etc.), one hog.

When getting out timber for the grave (*wubaw la ai*), one hog.

When clearing the jungle around the grave (*lup ra kanen ai*), one cow.

When building the structure over the grave, one bullock.

When separating the dead and the living (*măga măran ai*), one hog.

When dancing the final dance around the grave (*lup hkreng*), one fowl.

When the friends, the last evening, put the belongings of the deceased around the grave (*bunghkaw sa shădun ai*), a fowl and a pig.

Announcement of death. When anyone expires, the news is announced by the firing of guns and beating of gongs. This is especially true if it is a chief or some old respected person of the community. Distant friends and relatives are called to the funeral, and those near at hand repair to the house of mourning for the sake of seeing (*lăhpu yu ai*), the deceased, making presents, partaking of the sacrifices, and rendering assistance in such ways as they can. In the case of the demise of some prominent member of the community or a chief, usually all work is suspended for one or two days, but this is not compulsory except where there has been a death by accident.

Shrouding, washing and removing the corpse (*mang shăkru ai*). One of the first requisites is the bringing of water for washing the face of the corpse. Two men armed with guns proceed to the village spring followed by two women. One of them carries a bamboo vessel, the mouth of which is cut, contrary to custom, at the smaller end. (A Kachin cutting his bamboo vessels for the use of liquor or carrying of water, always makes the opening at the lower joint, counted from the root; but nearly everything connected with the burial (*lup măkoi*), is done up side down (*wutan ē*), to signify that the ways and customs among the departed are opposite to those of the living.) The two men fire their guns into the spring, forcing back the water, and as it rushes back again the woman with the bamboo vessel makes a plunge for the desired amount, and a hasty retreat is effected.

The shrouding takes place before the washing of the face. All the belongings in the line of clothing and ornaments are used. The dead body is dressed up as for an ordinary feast, and what cannot be worn is placed before the place occupied. But in order to indicate that the dead person is facing the other world, bag and sword are hung from the left shoulder instead of the right. The water is now brought in and is poured into an old, valued gong, if it is a chief, and into an ordinary gong if it is a commoner. The corpse is held seated on a low stool. A little of the water is poured in the left hand, which is passed over the face once only. To repeat it would be to follow the way of the living. Many Kachins never use their left hand in washing their face, since this is the way of the dead. As the washing is taking place, the onlookers and those attending to the details raise from time to time a loud, weird, or mournful lamentation.

While the deceased is still lying where he expired, a cow or a buffalo is brought opposite the place. A priest takes a sword and places it between himself and the corpse, and begins addressing the same. He tells the former lord of the house (or whatever the station may be), that he is now a spirit (*tsu*), and will be honored accordingly. He is requested not to speak to any of the inmates of the house, not to long for companions from the earth, and not to interfere in their pleasures. The animal is killed with a blow from the back of an ax just behind the horns. The carcass is divided into two equal parts, one for the dead and one for the living; but only old people can eat of this meat. So in order to enable all to partake, a fowl is substituted for the very old people and the dead. The head, wings and legs are placed before the corpse. The half of the regular sacrifice belonging to the dead is now divided. Parts are placed on the altar for the deceased, and all who have passed the child-bearing age can partake of the rest. Young and middle-aged people must not touch this part of the offering as it will make them indifferent to their posterity. The half for the living is divided and eaten by all the visitors, and small packages (*hkringbai*), are sent all around the village.

The body is now moved to the head of the chief fire-place, and is covered with at least two blankets. Children and near relatives come and pass their hands over the body, stripping it of imaginary belongings, and putting them into imaginary bags hung around the waist. This indicates that they wish to keep for themselves all the luck, good fortune and property possessed by the deceased, thus preventing him from carrying it away to the *nat*-country. The eyes of the departed are at this juncture closed by some particular friend. The belief is that as long as there is anything the deceased may still desire, the eyes will not close and the body will not grow cold or stiff. In some localities a piece of money is dropped into the mouth to enable the shade to pay the ferryman, but this is not a regular Kachin custom.

Placed in state, (*mang jang*). The dead having been properly attended to and thus satisfied (*shăkru*), and having been resting (*shărawn*), at the place of honor at the chief fire-place, a low sofa-like elevation of bamboo is put up at the *nat*-corner, and there the body is laid, and is curtained off from view. There it remains till the burial. But the spirit (*tsu*), from this moment becomes the guardian family *nat,* until it is sent off to the ancestral realms. The family altar is removed, and all the emblems of all the former *nats* who had a place there are put out of the way for the new occupant. A fire-place is made especially for the new *nat* by which to keep comfortable; food, not containing salt or pepper, is placed before him at least once a day, and in case of illness in the family, sacrifices are made to the new guardian imploring his help and assistance.

Making of the coffin (*dău daw ai*). The coffin of a chief is always made of the odina tree (a species of pinkadoe), (*lătsai hpun*); commoners must not use this kind, or they will encounter the offended spirits of their chieftains in the other world. The tree, whatever kind is used, is bought with a price; a fowl is dashed against the trunk when it is about to fall, in order to propitiate the genius of the tree for being put to such use. The fowl is eaten by those doing the work. A slab, half a foot in thickness, is split for the cover, the rest is hollowed out for the coffin. There is as a rule no attempt at ornamentation, and the coffin is daubed with red clay if the interment is several days off. In that case a small hole is made by the feet, connected with a bamboo pipe which conducts the secretions to a hole in the ground under the house. The burial always takes place on an even day after the demise. It must be on the second, fourth, sixth or eight day. Only a prophet is buried on the seventh day for reasons already explained.

The kăroi. Before every house of mourning is placed a circle of bamboos interspersed with branches of trees. Leaves and foliage must be left as it is, and the whole resembles a clump of bamboo, the upper circle being wider than the base. The whole is held together with strong bands of bamboo, rattan or vines cut from the jungle. The timber contained in this circle (*kăroi*), remains till the day when the hut over the grave is put up, and is used for this purpose. It must never be used for anything else. A bullock or a buffalo is offered when the *kăroi* is put up and articles of dress and ornaments are hung up around the fixture to remain for a day or two, or until after the burial.

The first part of the funeral dance, (*ndaw kăhkrang*). After the placing of the *kăroi,* a dance around the same takes place as a kind of introduction to the regular death-dance (*kăbung dum*), and the funeralc eremonies outside the house.

A cluster of bamboo around which Kachins dance when mourning.

A Karoi with large drum.

P. 200.

Two men especially familiar with all the details carry each a spear. One is representative of the living (*sut ndaw*), and the other of the spirits of the departed (*kătsan ndaw*). Ornaments of miniature baskets, tassels of red wool or yak's tails, small bells or coins, are hung on each of the spears. Everything connected with the spear of wealth (representing the living) is carefully attached and finished, while carelessness and hurry mark every detail regarding the other spear. When the dancing, a kind of strutting and prancing, begins, the man who carries the spear of wealth, holds it in the ordinary way, while the man with the other spear carries it the wrong end first, and thrusts it in every direction as he prances along. Having finished the prescribed rounds outside, a part of the program is enacted inside the house. It illustrates in a series of mimic acting the death, washing of the face, and other parts of the funeral ceremonies as already described. The two men are the sole actors while inside, but anyone can join in the prance outside. As the dance becomes more animated they go through a large number of convolutions and quick-steps, sometimes resembling a negro cake-walk, except that the two spears are very much in evidence and everyone is quiet and keeps a sober face.

The grave (*lup*). The place in which to dig a grave is ascertained by divination. In old communities where ancestral graves have been kept up, and a kind of cemetery has become the result, it is customary to bury near there, but this is not the ordinary way. Kachin graves are scattered all over the jungle, far or near from the village. When the grave is to be dug, someone takes an egg and blesses it, especially mentioning the name of the deceased. Then a party proceeds to some place where it is thought the departed may wish to be buried. The egg is thrown and if it breaks it is a sign that it is the proper place. If it does not break the first time repeated experiments are made in different places. If no egg is used, a long, low hill is selected which, in imagination, is fancied to resemble a human body. The high end is called the head, the lower part the feet. The rolling sides are the hands, any small protrusion is designated a table, and a level or small declivity is named a tray or server. The grave ascertained by the help of the egg is always dug so that the head is toward the house. In the other kind of grave the imaginary parts of the body determine the position. A fowl is killed and presented to the deceased before the grave is dug; this is afterwards eaten by the grave-diggers. The customary depth of a grave is up to the small of a man's back, and the earth must be carefully placed, as it all must be shovelled back into the grave. If there is enough for a small hill it is a good sign; if there is barely enough to cover the coffin, and packs so there is no hill, it is a sign that there will be no blessings from the deceased. He is in some way displeased and takes everything away to the other side.

The burial (*mang hta ai* or *lup măkoi*). The burial, as a rule, takes place on the fourth day, but if distant friends or relatives find it impossible to be present it may be postponed to the sixth or eighth day. No burial can take place on an odd day. Before the coffin is tied down children and relatives take a last look at the departed. On the lid are drawn rude figures of eyes, designed to frighten small children so they will stay away from the funeral. The belief is that the deceased, unwilling to separate from all his loved ones, may entice some of the young and innocent to follow him to the spirit land. In that case they will soon die. Returning from the grave the mourners break small twigs or branches from the surrounding bush, with which they brush away anything that may cling to them from contact with death, muttering a prayer that they may never have to go that way again. In some localities the coffin is opened at the grave to see if the corpse has moved the head; after being declared, "it has not moved," the burial takes place. Guns may be fired as the funeral procession moves on, when at the grave or returning, but this is a matter of local custom and individual pleasure. This closes the first and the least important part of the funeral ceremonies.

The second part. In some cases the body is kept above ground for weeks and months pending the final and more important ceremonies. The body disposed of, the spirit must await the final instructions. If the body is thus held, it is kept in the coffin as before described, or else, wrapped up in mats or bamboo casings, is hung in the jungle. It is not often that this happens nowadays; but in days gone by it was quite customary, especially among the well-to-do, who could afford to go through with all the ceremonies at once.

The death-dance, (*kăbung dum*). From the time of the burial to the day of the final ceremonies, the death-dance is danced nightly in the house of the deceased, unless the spirit has been put to sleep, awaiting the final obsequies. Three gongs of different sound and tonal power are used, and the dancing is in accordance with strict rules and regulations. The central idea is to afford pleasure for the departed and to remind him that he is honored and remembered. The dance is an intricate affair of stepping, prancing and shuffling, but every movement has a meaning. As a rule there are no less than thirty-seven different steps, movements and postures, representing everything in daily life appreciated by the dancers. The life they live, their pleasures, sorrows and misfortunes are all illustrated. The thought of death is prominently before them, but their aim and purpose is to drive away the dark side of the picture. The first part of the performance centers around the corpse. The looking at the dead, the washing, shrouding, etc., are all gone through in imagination. Then they go through the ordinary duties of house work, and in pantomime enact all the phases of clearing a paddy-field, planting, sowing and harvesting. The planting of beans and cotton, spinning and weaving, usually wind up the mimic performance. Some of the steps and postures are rather graceful, some are suggestive of the coarser side of their life. At intervals a loud, weird yell is raised, while the three gongs unceasingly send out their low, deep, mournful tones into the stillness of the night. It is especially the young people who join in the dance, but it is proper for old and young, men, women and children to swell the numbers. There are always two leaders, and all must change steps, postures and positions according to their direction. The origin of the dance is like every other custom referred back to ancestral times, and has been explained in the chapter on mythology and traditions, under the section *Origin of death.*

Putting the spirit to sleep (*tsu shăyup ai*). If the family is not financially able to perform the final ceremonies within a few months after the demise, or if there are other considerations why there should be delay, the spirit is put to sleep, with the promise that when the time comes he will be called and be properly conducted on the road to the ancestral realms. It is always an expensive affair to dispose of the spirit, and a great deal of preparation is necessary. An offering is made in connection with the ceremony of putting the *tsu* to sleep, and the spirit is exhorted to remain quietly in the *nat*-place until everything is in readiness for the final honors. The death-dance is suspended, and other attentions are withheld. In the meantime the village people gather wood and help in other preparations for the culminating event. When everything is ready the spirit is aroused, friends and relatives are called by two young men carrying spears, sacrifices are set aside, food and drink in abundance is provided, and the most important part of the obsequies takes place.

The hiding of the corpse, (*mang măkoi*). The actual burial may have taken place weeks, months or even years before the sending away of the spirit, still the final act is generally called *mang măkoi,* the hiding of the corpse. This is because the building of the structure over the grave, and the final honors around the same take place just before the spirit is sent on its last journey. While the spirit has been dwelling at the *nat*-place, it has not actually separated itself from the body in which it used to live; but after hiding the corpse the spirit takes its departure. There are thus two distinct ceremonies called by the same name and enacted at the same time.

On the morning of the eventful day a hog is killed with a blow from the back of an ax. After the sacrificial meal is over a short dance is danced outside the house, and all interested proceed to the jungle to cut timber for the structure over the grave, and prepare the customary objects for ornamentation. The day following a cow or a buffalo is killed, and from now on till the end of the ceremonies, as many cattle as the family can afford are slaughtered. The more the better both for the deceased and the family; the greater the sacrifice the greater the blessing. The timber being cut, the grave, which may be overgrown with jungle, is cleared and the structure is erected. Three kinds of graves are recognized: the bee-hive shape (*hkinchyang lup*), a shed without walls (*jărawp lup*), a cairn or a monumental casement of cut stone (*nlung lup*), usually put up by Chinese workmen. Chiefs claim the monopoly of the second kind, commoners have to be satisfied with the first, and only exceptionally wealthy people can afford the third. A rude figure of a human being is put on the top of the structure, and ornaments in various shapes representing birds or beasts or household articles are hung around on tall bamboo posts. But there are no strict rules as to these things, and a great deal is left to individual taste and fancy. The structure over the grave is usually completed on the third day, and the *kăroi* is torn down and the timber thus obtained is used where needed. After the completion of the hut a deep ditch (*lup hka*), is dug around the whole, signifying that the inmate from now on belongs to the other side and must not pass over to this. In case the departed has died in a feud, or been killed because of some grievance, the ditch is left incomplete until the law of a life for a life has been satisfied. Formerly some of these ditches were ten to fifteen feet deep and had a circumference of seventy-five to a hundred feet. The heads and horns of twenty, thirty or more buffaloes would be hung around on sacrificial poles, making known the great wealth and honor of the departed. But such elaborate affairs are not possible in these days of poverty and passing of the ancestral glory.

On the fourth day, as a rule, are enacted the final ceremonies around the grave. The final dance is performed by two men, and the gate to the enclosure is closed four times. The visitors again break small branches from the brush with which to brush off whatever may cling to them from the four days contact with the grave and death. This ends the ceremony of disposing of (hiding) the corpse, and the procession returns to the village to prepare for the final details in and around the house.

The final ceremonies at the house, (*shătsim ai lam*). Having returned from the grave, a bullock is killed and a sacrificial meal is prepared. There is a dance in front of the house, when branches are carried and flourished. Two men dressed as clowns amuse the public, often with immodest dancing and indecent songs and gestures, at the same time pretending to cry and mourn for the departed. They ask for all kinds of impossible gifts and presents, and after something of small value has been presented they are driven off amidst jeers and laughter. It is now about sunset and the last dance in front of the house takes place. The spears representing the now and the hereafter are removed. Offerings or presents are made to the priests. The final death-dance is enacted. Only eight persons participate, four on each side, guided by the two leaders. The holes for the bamboo poles of the *kăroi* are filled in. A priest takes a large seed of the *Entada pursaetha* (*shămyen*), and holding it in a pair of bamboo pincers roasts it in a slow fire. Then he cuts it in half and the piece that drops off belongs to the deceased. He is asked to take and plant it. If it grows he may be permitted to return to the former abode, otherwise he must remain in the spirit-world. This part of the ceremony is called *măga măran,* the separating of the dead and the living.

The sending away of the spirit (*tsu shăbawn dat ai*). Now that all the preliminaries have been performed, and the dead and the living have been separated, the most important part of all takes place. A priest tears down the bamboo elevation where the spirit has been abiding since the day of separation from the body. The timber is carried by a small party towards the grave, and is scattered along the road. Arriving at the grave for the last time a few things belonging to the departed are hung up to be removed the following morning. Then a garment (*măjip uba*), is thrown on the top of the grave, when a man picks it up and throws it back to the first man. This is repeated four times and then the party returns. Flour or ashes is scattered along the road, that the spirits of the living, who out of love or sympathy may follow the departed on his journey to the spirit-land, may find their way back. While this is going on outside the house a priest (*tsu dumsa*), has been leading the spirit on to the ancestral abodes. Holding a spear before him and stepping on a sword, he has exhorted the spirit to leave its place (*njang*), at the *nat*-corner, and follow the central post up to the house-ridge, and then depart by the front gable. Then over grass, brush and trees, hills and mountains, brooks and rivers, the road is shown until finally the white river (*uhpraw hka*), is reached which is the boundary between the now and the hereafter. The priest conducts the spirit across, exhorting it not to be afraid of the wild boars on each side, but changing appearance and putting on the forehead of a monkey pass nine cross-roads and at the tenth turn off to the ancestral realms. This in short is the outline of the formula it would take a whole night to rehearse, and with this the spirit as well as the corpse are disposed of, unless the spirit for some reason or other returns to its former home. In that case there is a new *nat* to honor, and fear and propitiate with sacrifices. How many of the gods and goddesses mentioned in history have had their origin similar to that of the Kachin *nats!* We read in this the history of many a religion and form of worship.

Sprinkling of the house of mourning. After the corpse has been hid, and the spirit has been sent away, the mourners, visitors, house and belongings of the deceased are sprinkled with water. The Fate of the mourners (*sinsu mǎraw*), is propitiated with a fowl. The spirits of those who out of love or sorrow have accompanied the departed to the new home among the shades, are formally recalled by a rather touching formula, being directed to return by the same road the deceased followed in departing. This part of the ceremony (*minla lǎlaw ai*), is usually followed by the blessing of the dreams (*yup mang shǎman ai*), that friends and relatives may have regarding the deceased and the funeral.

The last sign. The morning after the close of the ceremonies, some of the family return to the grave and if everything remains as left the evening before it is a sign that the departed is satisfied and has remained in spirit-land. But if anything has been touched, or tracks of animals are seen in the ashes or flour scattered along the road, the spirit has returned and there is another *nat* to account for. If all is satisfactory, the visitors pass their hands over the heads of the offerings hung around the grave, stripping them of such blessings and good fortune as the deceased has been pleased to bestow, and put them into imaginary bags. This being done, they return home and no further attention is paid to the grave. The structure or monument will in time decay or disappear and the grave will be overgrown with jungle and forgotten. In a few years it may be a part of a paddy-field.

The re-instatement of the household nats, (*nat kǎting ai*). The family *nats* who were suspended when the *tsu* took its place at the *nat*-altar are reinstated, and if the spirit has

Bamboo hut over a grave. P. 208

returned it takes its place in the pantheon. A grand dance (*poi du kălut mănau*), celebrates the return of the former divinities, in case the family can bear the expense. But considering the heavy drain on their resources in connection with the necessary proceedings, very few can bear this additional burden; and the family guardians are compelled to return without these extra honors. Some kinds of offerings are of course presented, and things will go on as before until the next time guns and drums and the three gongs announce another spirit on its way to the ancestral shades.

Death by violence or accident (*lăsa si*). The above is a description of the ceremonies where everything is in the regular order. But when the deceased has passed away by violence or accident, there are different rules and regulations. Such are not buried, but cremated; and the soul is not sent to the ancestral realm, but to the upper regions, to a place half way between earth and heaven, or to heaven itself. All persons killed in war, or such as have been killed by tigers, lightning or snake-bite, those who have been drowned or met death by falling from a tree, and women who have died in child-birth, have a place to themselves in what the Kachins call "heaven." A holiday of one day is declared when anyone in a community meets such a misfortune. It is regarded as a special visitation from Providence, probably for some particular mistake or offence.

While cremation among Kachins in general is practiced only in the cases mentioned, the Săsans in the Hukong valley burn (*ju*), all their dead. The custom has evidently been introduced from Assam, and indicates Hindu influence. The other families in that section do not follow this custom but bury in the usual way.

CHAPTER XVII.

THE FUTURE OF THE KACHINS.

The future of the hill tribes is bound up with the future of Burma. What this will be no one can predict; but that the Burma to come will know very little of the old Burmans, and will belong to a new people now in the advance admits of no controversy. The Burmans of the past have had their day, they have done their work, and are slowly but surely passing away. Burma is a melting pot where a new people with a new destiny is in the making. The large influx from China and India, to say nothing of the European influence, is creating new conditions. We may regret that an old civilization, admirably adapted for the peaceful life of a naturally happy and non-aggressive people, is passing away, but there is no way of recalling the past and the march of events is inevitable. As soon as an individual or a people fall behind in the Marathon race of history, the decree is written and can never be blotted out. A dying race, like a dying man, may linger on for some time, but the old time vigor and strength can never be restored. It does not matter if it is the Assyrian, Roman or Burman, the law is the same for all.

The backward races of Burma feel the pressure of the modern life, and some of them, especially among the Karens, are doing their best to adjust themselves to the new order of things. But this is an age of consolidation, and the individual will sooner or later be lost in the mass. Small tribes and groups of races cannot long maintain their particular characteristics and peculiarities. Many of the Karens are fast becoming Burmanized, in the sense that they use Burmese as their everyday language, while in other respects they are moulded by western influence. Education, and the new life it brings, is rapidly changing lower Burma, and it is only a question of time when the same forces will be felt in every part of the province. China will take its place among the strong nations of the world, and her influence on Burma, which has always been great, will be still more marked. It is from this source that the Kachins, and other northern tribes, will be most largely influenced, but there are today some movements on hand worthy of consideration.

Respect for law. The Kachins have now for a quarter of a century felt the strong hand of British rule, and they are just beginning to realize that the past will not return. They can no longer acquire new territory by conquest; they cannot raid, rob or levy blackmail on the lowlands; they must live in peace with all men and do honest work for their living. What this means for a naturally predatory people is easy to see. They must work harder than ever before and still have far less than they were used to. It cannot be denied that they are much poorer than in days gone by, and that life is to them much more of a burden. This is the hard school in which they have been placed. As a race they have not been able to adjust themselves to the new conditions; most of them have refused to make an attempt, hoping that there would be some change in their favor, and some of them are hopelessly incapable of doing it. They are probably slightly on the increase, but no reliable figures are available. The census report is inadequate, and the Kachins will do all in their power to withhold information. They do not understand the nature of the census, always being under the impression that it is only the forerunner to increased taxation. But all these things have an educational value, and gradually they will learn to appreciate peace with hard work, and forget the ease which war and plunder formerly brought.

Education. Several hundred Kachins, (probably by this time there may be over a thousand), have for longer or shorter periods been in the Kachin schools. The mission schools in Bhamo, Myitkyina and Namhkam have educated by far the largest number, and today have under their care about four hundred pupils. Another hundred may be found in Government schools and Buddhist monasteries. Most of the pupils in the mission schools become Christians, and those who do not unite with a Christian church, are always friendly to new ideas. Still the Kachins have not been as receptive or accessible as for instance the Karens. Only a comparatively small number have accepted Christianity, and still fewer have embraced Buddhism. They cling to their old religion because it is "the custom," and has been handed down by their forefathers, firmly believing that whatever may be its defects it is the best for them. The inconvenience of a change with its effects on the tribal and family relations, together with a natural conservatism, are the greatest obstacles in the way. After thirty-five years or more of mission work among them, the churches count about four hundred communicants, while the adherents would be three times that number. Very few of the really leading families have accepted the new faith. It is mostly the poor and the needy that have come, naturally with a view to improving their economic conditions, when giving up their own expensive form of religion.

The Kachin language having been reduced to writing, there is the beginning of a literature, and the number able to read and write is constantly on the increase. So far all the books printed are, with two exceptions, of a religious nature, and for the advance of the Christian religion and a Christian education. Most likely the Kachin literature will never be large. Most of those who learn to read will also acquire Burmese, and thus come in contact with a richer store of knowledge.

The Military Police. Several hundred young men from all parts of Kachin land have served in the Kachin Military Police, and thus come in contact with a side of life unknown to them before. This too has been, and is, a civilizing agency. The military discipline, the necessity of doing things according to rules and orders, are things new to the lawless hill-men, and must have a wholesome effect. Many of them have also in the barracks learned to read the written Kachin, and acquired other useful knowledge. Thus when returning to their mountain homes they carry with them new ideas of the world and its ways. That many of them have also learned things far from desirable is no doubt true; but the good and the bad often goes hand in hand.

These influences are doing their work quietly, but surely. A Kachin people is growing up in ways unknown to their forefathers. They will identify themselves with the larger life of upper Burma. As they accept more of a Christian education, and leave their old superstitions behind them, the natural advance will be towards a Christian civilization.

SUPPLEMENT.

I. TERMS OF RELATIONSHIP.

---

1. For the use of some of these terms in different persons and numbers, see the Kachin Grammar § 27.

2. Terms of relationship have a wider application than with us. Thus a man's brothers would call his father-in-law by the same appellation as he himself.

Aji ni, Paternal ancestors.

Awoi ni, Maternal ancestors.

Dama, (1) A husband's relatives; (2) all tribal families with which intermarriage is allowed, viewed from the male side; (3) sometimes used as a respectful term for a son-in-law.

Di, A paternal uncle, older than the father.

Dim, A paternal uncle younger than the father.

Doi, A paternal uncle younger than the *dim.*

Dwi ke, A maternal great-grandmother, a mother's father's mother.

Gu, (1) A father-in-law, a husband's father; (2) a brother-in-law, a husband's elder brother; (3) a paternal aunt's (*moi a*) husband, or brothers; (4) a brother-in-law, used by a wife's younger sister; (5) an uncle, when addressed by the wife's brother's children.

Gaida, A widow; also called *gaida jan.*

Jan, A sister (generally thought of as a younger sister), of a man.

Ji, See *aji ni:* a grandfather, see *ji hkai.*

Ji dwi, A maternal grandfather.

Ji ke, A paternal great-grandfather.

Ji ke dwi, A maternal great-grandfather.

Ji hkai, A paternal grandfather.

Ji woi, Ancestors, viewed collectively.

Hkau, (1) Cousins, a paternal aunt's male children when

addressing the mother's nephew and vice versa; (2) a brother-in-law, a wife's brother, used on both sides; (3) a polite term between young men of equal age and standing.

Hkai dwi, Same as *woi dwi,* but more respectful.

Hkri, (1) Cousins, a paternal aunt's (*moi a*) female children; (2) a paternal aunt's husband's sisters; (3) the children of a sister, either a nephew or niece ; (4) a son-in-law; (5) a respectful compellation used by a man when addressing a women of equal age and standing, not being a relative.

Ma, A child.

Moi, (1) A paternal aunt, a father's sister whether younger or older; (2) a mother-in-law, a husband's mother.

Mădu jan, A wife.

Mădu wa, A husband.

Măyu, (1) A wife's relatives; (2) all tribal families with which intermarriage is allowed, and from which wives may be taken.

Măyu dama, Relations in general; see parts.

Na, (1) An elder sister; (2) a husband's elder brother's wife, a sister-in-law; (3) cousins, an uncle's or aunt's female children older than the speaker; (4) a respectful and friendly compellation addressed to a female acquaintance older than the speaker.

Nam, (1) A sister-in-law, a wife's younger sister; (2) a sister-in-law, used by a husband's elder brother; (3) a daughter-in-law; (4) the children of a brother-in-law; (5) a nephew or niece, a wife's brother's children.

Ni, (1) A mother-in-law, a wife's mother; also the mother-in-law's sisters, (2) a wife's brother's wife, a sister-in-law.

Ning, (1) A sister-in-law, a husband's sister; (2) a wife when addressed by the husband's aunts; (3) a compellation between women of equal age and standing addressed in the way of affection or friendship.

Nu, A mother.

Nan, (1) A younger brother or sister; (2) cousins, an uncle's or aunt's children younger than the speaker; (3) a brother-in-law, a wife's younger sister's husband; (4) a sister-in-law, a man's younger brother's wife.

Ndoi, (1) A mother's younger sister, an aunt; (2) a father's younger brother's wife.

N-gyi, A bastard.

Hpu, (1) An elder brother; (2) cousins, an uncle's or aunt's male children older than the speaker; (3) a brother-in-law, woman's elder sister's husband.

Rat, (1) A sister-in-law, a wife's elder sister, addressed by her husband or vice versa. (2) an elder brother's wife; (3) a husband's younger brother.

Sha, A child, a son, or a daughter. (2) a nephew or niece, a wife's younger sister's children.

Shingkra, A widower.

Shu, (1) A grandchild; (2) a sister's children's (*hkri ni a*) husbands and children; (3) an affectionate term used by old people to children.

Shu măshi, Descendants of the third generation.

Shu măsha, Descendants of the fourth generation.

Shu măshi,
Shu măsha, } Generation after generation.

Shădang sha, A son.

Shăyi sha, A daughter.

Tung, (1) A mother's elder sister, a maternal aunt; (2) a father's elder brother's wife.

Tsa, (1) An uncle, a mother's brother whether younger or older; (2) a father-in-law, the wife's father; (3) a respectful compellation used by a woman when speaking to a man of equal age and standing.

Wa, A father.

Wa di, (1) An uncle, a father's elder brother; (2) a mother's elder sister's (*Tung a*) husband; (3) a respectful designation when addressing an elderly man.

Wa doi, (1) An uncle, a father's younger brother; (2) a mother's younger sister's (*Ndoi a*) husband.

Woi, See *awoi ni.*

Woi dwi, A maternal grandmother; see ***hkai dwi.***

Woi ke, A paternal great-grandmother.
Woi ke dwi, A maternal great-grandmother
Woi hkai, A paternal grandmother.

II. FAMILY NAMES. (Comp. Chap. I.)

There are, as has been pointed out in our first chapter, no subdivisions to the families of the chiefs. But this does not mean that there are no descendants among the commoners from the ruling families. Naturally there has always been a downward tendency from the chief families. The succession has been perpetuated through the youngest son, and his brothers had to find a place in the community the best they could, or else by conquest establish their authority in new directions. Those unable to do so soon found themselves on a level with commoners and after two or three generations they lost the old family name and took on a new. For example the Dămau family was formerly called Săhkung, and they came from a branch of the Mărip family; the Dashi family come directly from the Lăhtaws. Hundreds of families, if they go back far enough, can trace their pedigree to a family of chieftains, but today they carry the name of commoners and are regarded as such.

Names of localities, or as we would say circles or districts, have often suggested the name for a new family; but in many instances the local designation has nothing to do with family relations. The large Lăhpai family for example, rule the whole of the Atsi country, the Gauri hills, the Hpunggan and Găra communities and the Mongsi (Monggyi) valley. It is incorrect to speak of a "Gauri Lăhpai," as though the word Gauri applied to the Lăhpai only. The Nangzing or Mălang families of commoners are just as much Gauris as the Lăhpai family of chiefs. In this case the whole circle has apparently taken its name from an influential family of commoners. The Gauri family is now small but was formerly in the lead. The name Atsi is today given a large clan, ruled by Lăhpai chiefs. Originally it may have been the name of a single family or of some locality.

The same family may be divided into a number of smaller divisions. Thus the Hpau family (apparently sprung from the Lăhtaws), has at least seventeen subdivisions or branches.

The same family may carry different names in different sections of the country. Thus the Lăbang family (descendants of the Nhkums, are called in Hkahku land Dutsan, and in the Hukong valley Săsan.

We do not intend to give an exhaustive list of family names. It would be of no practical value. Some families are nearly extinct; new ones are constantly growing up, and new names may be applied to one or more branches of an old lineage. What may be a nickname today descriptive of some locality, event or personal peculiarity, will after a few years be recognized as a family name. Thus a branch of the Săhkung family came to be called Dămau, because a certain old man placed (*da*) a new altar to the *mau nat* (Atsi for *mu*) at the gable of his house, a thing no one had ever done before. All that we regard as essential is, (1) the names of the ruling families; (2) some of the local names designating their districts, and (3) the names of the leading families among their subjects. Commoners who trace their lineage to one or the other of the ruling families will be indicated by placing the ancestral name in parentheses.

I. The five ruling families:

Mărip, Lăhtaw, Lăhpai, Nhkum, Măran.

II. Some of the names indicating territorial divisions:

(*1*) *Mărip:*

Kansi, Sinli, Singdung, Ningtun, Tingrun.

(*2*) *Lăhtaw:*

Ningtup, Săna, Tingra, Wala, Mong-ya.

(*3*) *Lăhpai:*

Atsi, Gauri, Găra, Mongsi, Hpunggan. Htama, Sadan.

(4) *N-Hkum :*

Mong Baw, Watau, Săsan.

(5) *Măran :*

Laika, Lăna.

III. Leading families among the commoners :

Aura, (*Gauri*)	*Chyanhpn,*	*Dingga,*
Bama (*Nhkum*)	*Dăbang* (*Maru*)	*Dun,* (*Nhkum*)
Băla	*Damang,*	*Dauji,* (*Nhkum*)
Bălu,	*Dashi,* (*Lahtaw*)	*Dama,* (*Măru*)
Chyamnut,	*Dingdu,*	*Dămau,* (*Mărip*)
Chyangyi,		
Gumtung,	*Lăsum,*	*Păsi,*
Gauri,	*Lăzing,*	*Păsham,*
Gawtu, (*Marip*)	*Lăzum,*	*Hpaudau,*
Găra,	*Lăshi,*	*Hpaugan,*
Jangma,	*Maida,*	*Hpaujang,*
Kambau,	*Măbwi,*	*Hpauje,*
Kangda,	*Măgau,*	*Hpaujum,*
Kangma,	*Mălu,* (*Lahtaw*)	*Hpaujung,*
Kumpyen,	*Mălang,*	*Hpaukun,*
Kumshaa,	*Mănam,*	*Hpauhkan,*
Kumting,	*Mărau,*	*Hpaula,*
Kaigyi	*Măraw,*	*Hpaulu,*
Kăreng,	*Măhtu,*	*Hpaulawn,*
Hkangda,	*Măshan,*	*Hpaumai,*
Hkangii,	*Măwehku,*	*Hpaunat,*
Hkuntang.	*Măwi hkaw,*	*Hpaushwi,*
Hkăna, (*Atst*)	*Măwe hpu,*	*Hpaushu,*
Hkrap,	*Myet shi,*	*Hpauyam,*
Lamai,	*Myiltung,* (*Măsip*)	*Hpauyawn,*
Lasang,	*Nangzing,*	*Sumnut,*
Lukna,	*Ningdup,*	*Lăbaw,*
Lumyang, (*Atsi*)	*Ninggu,* (*Nhkum*)	*Săgaw,*
Lawhkum, (*Lăhtaw*)	*Ninggyi,*	*Săhkung,* (*Marip*)
Lăung,	*Ninglam,*	*Săsan,*
Lăbang, (*Nhkum*)	*Ninglaw,*	*Shădau,* (*Mărip*)
Lăbya,	*Ningtap,*	*Shanghting,*

Lăchyung,	*Ningtuug,* (*Măran*)	*Tsinyu,*
Lăkang,	*Ningrung,* (*Mărip*)	*Tsinkrang,*
Lăhkum, (*Lăhpai*)	*Ningsnang,*	*Htingrin,*
Lăhkung,	*Nbăwi,*	*Waehye,*
LLăma, (*Nhkum*)	*Nbrang,*	*Wahpai,*
Lămung,	*Ndau,*	*Wurung,*
Lămau,	*Pala,*	*Yawngdeng,* (*Nhkum*)
Lăna,	*Padma,* (*Nhkum*)	*Linghtung,*
Lăsi,	*Pămang,*	

TOPICAL INDEX.

For EU product safety concerns, contact us at Calle de José Abascal, 56–1°,
28003 Madrid, Spain or eugpsr@cambridge.org.

www.ingramcontent.com/pod-product-compliance
Ingram Content Group UK Ltd.
Pitfield, Milton Keynes, MK11 3LW, UK
UKHW010344140625
459647UK00010B/813

* 9 7 8 1 1 0 8 0 4 6 0 9 1 *